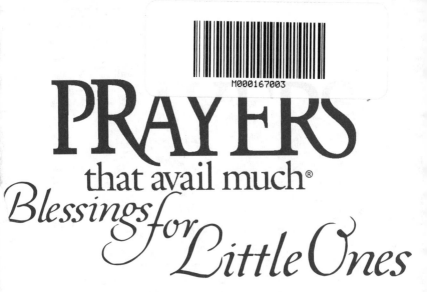

PRAYERS
that avail much®
Blessings for Little Ones

Germaine COPELAND

Charisma
HOUSE
A STRANG COMPANY

Most STRANG COMMUNICATIONS/CHARISMA HOUSE/SILOAM products are available at special quantity discounts for bulk purchase for sales promotions, premiums, fund-raising, and educational needs. For details, write Strang Communications/ Charisma House/Siloam, 600 Rinehart Road, Lake Mary, Florida 32746, or telephone (407) 333-0600.

PRAYERS THAT AVAIL MUCH®: BLESSINGS FOR LITTLE ONES
by Germaine Copeland
Published by Charisma House
A Strang Company
600 Rinehart Road
Lake Mary, Florida 32746
www.charismahouse.com

Unless otherwise noted, all Scripture quotations are from the New King James Version of the Bible. Copyright © 1979, 1980, 1982 by Thomas Nelson, Inc., publishers. Used by permission.

Scripture quotations marked NIV are from the Holy Bible, New International Version. Copyright © 1973, 1978, 1984, International Bible Society. Used by permission.

Cover design by Rachel Campbell

Library of Congress Cataloging-in-Publication Data
Copeland, Germaine.
    Prayers that avail much : blessings for little ones / Germaine Copeland.
        p. cm.
    Includes bibliographical references.
    ISBN 1-59185-606-X
1. Prayers. 2. Benediction. 3. Children--Religious life. I. Title.
    BV283.C5C65 2004
    242'.62--dc22
                                                          2004007448

04 05 06 07 08 — 987654321

I dedicate this book to our grandchildren:

Matthew, Joseph, Rachel, and Leah Copeland

Martha Jean Houser

Christopher Bone

Chandler Grace, Griffin, Emma Beam, Katherine Sutton

May your good deeds glow for all to see.

Contents

Welcome to Prayers That Avail Much®: Blessings for Little Ones. Words shape our destinies and the destinies of our children. Parents, the blessings that you read to your child from this book will pave the way for him or her to know the God of creation—the God who loves him, chose him, and planned his life before the foundation of the world.

My parents were the very first people I heard utter a prayer. We prayed on bended knee in the morning and evening. My father closed each night's prayer with, "Lord, we thank You for the angels who are encamped round about our home to watch over and protect us." We went to bed comforted and unafraid.

Often the Holy Spirit reminds me of the Word that was either read to me or prayed for me. Our children will grow up and make decisions that will not always please us. However, we can know that regardless of the obstacles each one faces, the Word of God will light his pathway. He will hear a voice saying, "This is the way. Walk in it." When he goes out, he will not be lost.

God made a covenant with Abraham and declared, "And I will establish My covenant between Me and you and your descendants after you in their generations, for an everlasting covenant, to be God to you and your descendants after you" (Gen. 17:7).

Through the work of Christ Jesus, God has blessed the Gentiles with the same blessing He promised to Abraham (Gal. 3:14). You have the ability to pass these blessings on to your child.

This book is intended to inspire parents and caregivers to bless aloud their little ones. The blessings recorded in this book are intended for you as parents to speak and pray before the heavenly Father in the hearing of your child; they can be repeated as he matures. Give him Jesus—give him Life! Even though he may not intellectually comprehend the true meaning, his memory is recording all that he hears. Your child is spirit, soul, and body, and he is internalizing the words he hears. The Holy Spirit will give him understanding as he develops. The entrance of God's Word gives light.

I encourage you to pray in the hearing of your child every day. Speaking words that are spirit and life will elevate your thinking from the temporal to the eternal. God will give you the wisdom to train up your child in the way that he should go.

Prepare your child for his future so that his faith will not fail him when he has to move mountains. God is watching over His Word to perform it. The Word of God that you speak will not return void. God will not fail one word of His promise. You will be encouraged and built up spiritually as you read and meditate on the blessings contained in the following pages. Be blessed!

Welcome to the Family

Welcome to God's Family

What a wonderful day it is to welcome a new child into the family! The psalmist wrote, "Behold, children are a heritage from the LORD, the fruit of the womb is a reward. Like arrows in the hand of a warrior, so are the children of one's youth. Happy is the man who has his quiver full of them; they shall not be ashamed, but shall speak with their enemies in the gate" (Ps. 127:3–5).

As the parent of a little one, God has placed in your care a young child that He created in His own image. The days ahead will be full of the joys of that first smile, first word, first tooth, and first step. All of these are part of your child's journey toward receiving Jesus Christ as his personal Lord and Savior and fulfilling the destiny for which God created him.

Of course, the great honor of being a parent also comes with great responsibility. As your child begins his journey in the life that lies before him, his needs for food, shelter, love, protection, and guidance must be met if he is to be physically and emotionally healthy. However, it is important to remember that your child's needs do not stop there. His welfare is also dependent upon his spiritual needs being met. "Telling to the generation to come the praises of the LORD, and His strength and His wonderful works that He has done" (Ps. 78:4).

Fortunately, only one day comes at a time, and you are not alone. You have a Comforter, a Helper, who will guide you into all truth. In John 15:26 Jesus speaks of the Holy Spirit when He says, "But when the Helper comes, whom I shall send to you from the Father, the Spirit of truth who proceeds from the Father, He will testify of Me."

The happiest home is one that is a house of prayer, a place where your days together begin and end with prayer, praises to God, and spoken words of blessing. In fact, your very life can be a prayer to God; each moment can be an expression of thanksgiving and praise to Him. "So we, Your people and sheep of Your pasture, will give You thanks forever; we will show forth Your praise to all generations" (Ps. 79:13).

Your family will be knit together in faith, joy, and love when you set aside a time each day to pray, praise, and thank God and to speak words of life and blessing over your child. Because the blessings and prayers in this book are taken from the Word of God, you will be anchored together in Truth.

We can begin to see the importance of this by looking at Jesus' expression of His own love for the

3

little children. In Isaiah 40:11 we see a beautiful picture of Jesus and His little lambs: "He will gather the lambs with His arm, and carry them in His bosom." Then in Mark 10:16 we see this same picture: "And He took them [the children] up in His arms, laid His hands on them, and blessed them." Because He has entrusted you as the parent of His little lamb, you have been given the wonderful opportunity to stand in the Lord's stead over your child. You are Jesus' arms when you take your precious child in your arms; you are Jesus' hands when you lay your hands on him; you are Jesus' mouth when you speak words of life and truth over him.

Not only will your words and prayers release blessings to your child, but these words will also be a lamp unto your own feet. They will remind you of the wonderful plans God has for your child and for your family. The blessings, prayers, and Scripture readings will give you vision and clarity, and they will deepen your understanding of your purpose as a parent. They will give you a standard by which to live. They will bring to remembrance the splendors and wonders of God, thereby igniting joy, thanksgiving, and faith.

Day 1

My precious child, I love you and welcome you to our family. You were created for God's good pleasure. Long before God laid down earth's foundations, He had you in mind. He settled on you as the focus of His love.

SCRIPTURE READING

Blessed is every one who fears the LORD,
Who walks in His ways....
You shall be happy, and it shall be well with
  you.
Your wife shall be like a fruitful vine
In the very heart of your house,
Your children like olive plants
All around your table.
Behold, thus shall the man be blessed
Who fears the LORD.

—PSALM 128:1–4

Day 2

You are a heritage from God. You are my reward—a perfect gift sent to me from the Father above. He chose you to fulfill His divine destiny and bring glory to Him.

Day 3

Little one, God watched you from conception to birth. All the stages of your life are spread out before the Lord. He prepared the days of your life before you even lived one day. I bless you and ask the Father to lead you forth in peace.

SCRIPTURE READING

For You formed my inward parts;
You covered me in my mother's womb.
I will praise You, for I am fearfully and won-
    derfully made;
Marvelous are Your works,
And that my soul knows very well.

—PSALM 139:13–14

Day 4

Our heavenly Father loves you, and He has given you the grace to love Him. You will grow in the nurture and admonition of the Lord. You are His instrument of peace, filled with compassion for the less fortunate.

Day 5

When you hear the Word of God, mercy and truth will be written upon the tablets of your heart. The Father will bless you to find favor and good understanding with God and with man. The Lord gives you safety and eases you day by day.

SCRIPTURE READING

Let not mercy and truth forsake you;
Bind them around your neck,
Write them on the tablet of your heart,
And so find favor and high esteem
In the sight of God and man.

—PROVERBS 3:3–4

Day 6

You are created to be a disciple of Christ. You will be taught of the Lord and obedient to God's will because you are growing in the grace and knowledge of our Lord and Savior Jesus Christ. I commit you into God's hands, positively persuaded that God is able to keep that which I have committed to Him.

Day 7

I thank God for giving His angels charge over you to accompany, defend, and preserve you in all your ways. God is your refuge and fortress. He is the glory and the lifter of your head.

SCRIPTURE READING

I will say of the LORD, "He is my refuge and
   my fortress;
My God, in Him I will trust."...
For He shall give His angels charge over you,
To keep you in all your ways.

—PSALM 91:2, 11

Day 8

I pray for good fortune in everything you do and for your good health, so that your everyday affairs will prosper as well as your soul! Nothing will make me happier than knowing that you will continue diligently in the way of Truth!

Day 9

I commit to teach you God's ways, to help you listen and hear instruction, to help you pay attention and gain understanding. You will lay hold of God's words with all of your heart, and you will keep God's Word.

SCRIPTURE READING

Hear, my children, the instruction of a father,
And give attention to know understanding;...
"Let your heart retain my words;
Keep my commands, and live."
—PROVERBS 4:1, 4

Day 10

God has provided for everything you could possibly need, and He has abounded toward you with all prudence and wisdom. You will learn to be wise. You will develop good judgment and common sense! You will love and cling to Wisdom—she will protect and guard you in the name of Jesus.

Day 11

In Jesus' name I bless you and pray that you will find grace in God's eyes. His grace is sufficient for any situation, and He will give you courage to overcome every obstacle. I ask God to create in you the desire to be ever learning, ever growing, and ever achieving as you grow in the grace and the knowledge of our Lord Jesus Christ.

SCRIPTURE READING

He shall cover you with His feathers,
And under His wings you shall take refuge;...
You shall not be afraid of the terror by night,
Nor of the arrow that flies by day.
—PSALM 91:4–5

Day 12

Always remember that the Father is watching over you whether we are together or apart. He covers you with His feathers, and under His wings you shall take refuge. He will never leave you or forsake you. You are never alone.

Day 13

The Father God has provided blessings from heaven above. He will continue to bless you with every blessing in heaven because you are being prepared, pure and clean for God.

SCRIPTURE READING

Listen, for I will speak of excellent things,
And from the opening of my lips will come
   right things;
For my mouth will speak truth;
Wickedness is an abomination to my lips.
—PROVERBS 8:6–7

Day 14

Our God made your mouth to praise Him. He helps me teach you to speak of excellent things. The opening of your lips will be for right things, and you will say what is good and helpful to others.

Day 15

Father God has sent angels before you to keep and guard you on the way and to lead you to the destiny He has prepared for you. You are God's workmanship, created in Christ Jesus to do good works, which He prepared in advance for you to do.

SCRIPTURE READING

For we are His workmanship, created in Christ Jesus for good works, which God prepared beforehand that we should walk in them.
—EPHESIANS 2:10

Day 16

The Lord has sent the Holy Spirit who imparts wisdom, ability, understanding, intelligence, knowledge, and all kinds of craftsmanship to you for His glory. He is directing your education so that you will be strong, healthy, well read in many fields, well informed, alert, sensible, and poised before your teachers and peers.

Day 17

By the grace of God you are developing a desire to keep the way of the Lord by doing what is right and just, and He will bring about what He has promised. You will bring glory to the Father by living according to His ways.

Scripture Reading

All your children shall be taught by the
   LORD,
And great shall be the peace of your children.
In righteousness you shall be established;
You shall be far from oppression, for you shall
   not fear.

—Isaiah 54:13–14

Day 18

You will walk in the merciful Father's ways so that you will live safely and peacefully in a fruitful land. God's grace enables you to walk in all the ways that He has commanded you, so that you may live, prosper, and prolong your days on earth.

Day 19

I ask the Lord to bless you and keep you, to show you His kindness and to have mercy on you. I thank Him for watching over you and giving you peace. I ask the Lord God to give you the ability to see obstacles and challenges through eyes of faith. By His power, He has made you more than able to overcome.

SCRIPTURE READING

For God has not given us a spirit of fear, but of power and of love and of a sound mind.
—2 TIMOTHY 1:7

Day 20

I pray to the Lord that you will not turn aside to the right hand or to the left. I ask Him to give you a heart to walk in all His ways that He has commanded you so that you may live, that it may be well with you, and that He will prolong your days on earth.

Day 21

I ask the Father to give you a wise mind and spirit that is attuned to His will so that you may acquire a thorough understanding of the ways in which He works. May you choose to do what is true and fair and find all the good paths!

SCRIPTURE READING

For this reason we also, since the day we heard it, do not cease to pray for you, and to ask that you may be filled with the knowledge of His will in all wisdom and spiritual understanding; that you may walk worthy of the Lord, fully pleasing Him, being fruitful in every good work and increasing in the knowledge of God.

—COLOSSIANS 1:9–10

Day 22

I ask the Lord to give you insight to do what He tells you. May your whole life be one long, obedient response. I pray that you will store His words in your heart and soul, binding them as a sign on your hands and keeping them ever before your eyes.

Day 23

God has given you an obedient heart, so you will learn obedience and carefully obey Him by obeying your parents and teachers. Because you are obedient, the blessings of the Lord will come upon you, and you will eat the best from the land.

SCRIPTURE READING

Bless his substance, LORD, and accept the work of his hands.

—DEUTERONOMY 33:11

Day 24

I pray for the Lord to bless your skills and be pleased with the work of your hands. I thank God for creating a desire in you to work, to do something useful with your own hands so you may have something to share with those in need.

Day 25

God made you strong and very courageous. You will have success wherever you go as you act according to the Word of God. May the words of your mouth and the meditation of your heart be pleasing in the Lord's sight. He is your Rock and your Redeemer.

SCRIPTURE READING

Only be strong and very courageous, that you may observe to do according to all the law which Moses My servant commanded you; do not turn from it to the right hand or to the left, that you may prosper wherever you go.

—JOSHUA 1:7

Day 26

Always revere and respect the Lord; serve Him and hearken to His voice. He is creating in you an obedient heart so you will not rebel against Him. Following the Lord your God is a good thing!

Day 27

Together we praise the Lord for showing you His kindness and faithfulness. You will develop, growing up in all ways, and the Lord God will reveal His greatness to you. There is none like Him, nor is there any God besides Him. His way is holy! No god is great like our God!

SCRIPTURE READING

The righteous shall flourish like a palm tree,
He shall grow like a cedar in Lebanon.
Those who are planted in the house of the
    LORD
Shall flourish in the courts of our God.
—PSALM 92:12–13

Day 28

God is giving you an understanding heart to discern between good and evil. As you mature and practice doing what is right, you will learn right from wrong.

Day 29

I pray that God will give you rest and peace in all areas of your life and that He will keep evil far from you. Evil cannot come close to you; it cannot get through the door because God has ordered His angels to guard you wherever you go.

SCRIPTURE READING

No evil shall befall you,
Nor shall any plague come near your dwelling;
For He shall give His angels charge over you,
To keep you in all your ways.

—PSALM 91:10–11

Day 30

God did not give you a spirit of fear. Because those who are with you are more than those who are against you, you will not be afraid. I thank God for giving angels special charge over you to accompany, defend, and preserve you in all your ways of obedience and service to Him.

Day 31

May the Lord give you an understanding of the times. He chose you before the foundation of the world for such a time as this. He planned the paths on which you should walk. With praise and thanksgiving, you will sing to the Lord, saying, "You are good; Your love endures forever." You will praise God's name in song and glorify Him with thanksgiving.

SCRIPTURE READING

He chose us in Him before the foundation of the world, that we should be holy and without blame before Him in love....For we are His workmanship, created in Christ Jesus for good works, which God prepared beforehand that we should walk in them.

—EPHESIANS 1:4; 2:10

God's
Protection

Parental Blessings

We do not have to look far to find accounts of parents blessing their own children. Examples of this include Noah blessing two of his sons (Gen. 9:26–27), Isaac blessing his sons (Gen. 27:27–29, 39–40; 28:3–4), and the words of blessing that Jacob spoke over his sons (Gen. 49:1–28). In each case, these patriarchs of the faith spoke words of prophecy that the Lord had revealed would happen to their children. If we study the Scriptures, we find that in each case the words these men spoke over their sons did indeed come to pass.

If we look at Hebrews 11:20–21, we see that speaking a blessing over our children is an act of faith. It was by faith that Isaac blessed his own sons: "By faith Isaac blessed Jacob and Esau concerning things to come" (v. 20). It was also by faith that Jacob blessed Joseph's sons: "By faith Jacob, when he was dying, blessed each of the sons of Joseph, and worshiped, leaning on the top of his staff" (v. 21).

Both of these men spoke the words the Lord laid upon their hearts in advance of the events occurring. In Hebrews 11:39 we are told that these men were commended for their faith.

In turn, we can also bind our faith to the Word of God when we speak blessings over our own children and grandchildren. We have been given the written Word of God, and we can stand steadfast in faith that what is written in the Scriptures will indeed come to pass in the lives of our children. When we speak blessings that are based upon the Word of God, we are agreeing with the Word of God. Just as the patriarchs spoke out in faith that what the Lord had revealed to their hearts would come to pass, we can speak the Word of the Lord that has been revealed in the Scriptures and by His Spirit.

As you speak the Word of the Lord over your own child, praise God and thank Him for His mighty deeds and for what He is going to do in the life of your child and in your family as a whole. The Word of God is sure and true. You can depend upon it. "Above all, you must understand that no prophecy of Scripture came about by the prophet's own interpretation. For prophecy never had its origin in the will of man, but men spoke from God as they were carried along by the Holy Spirit" (2 Pet. 1:20–21, NIV).

As you speak blessings over your child, you can be confident that the Word of the Lord will indeed come to pass and that His Word will not come back void to Him.

Day 1

I pray that you will walk straight, act right, and tell the truth. I thank the Lord that you will obtain grace and favor in His sight. He is a sun and shield. He bestows favor and honor, and He will not withhold any good thing from you. His grace is sufficient for you, dear child. His power is made perfect in weakness.

SCRIPTURE READING

And He said to me, "My grace is sufficient for you, for My strength is made perfect in weakness." Therefore most gladly I will rather boast in my infirmities, that the power of Christ may rest upon me....For when I am weak, then I am strong.

—2 CORINTHIANS 12:9–10

Day 2

I ask God to create a hunger for His Word in your heart. His Word will thrill you, and you will be nourished by Scripture day and night. I thank God for shielding you on all sides, for grounding your feet, and for lifting your head high. The Lord God is your strength and your shield. Your heart will trust in the Lord, and He will help you in every situation.

Day 3

God is with you wherever you go. He will protect you and bring you back safely. He is with you constantly, giving you all He has promised. The Father's face radiates with joy because of you. He is gracious, and He will show you His favor and give you His peace.

SCRIPTURE READING

The LORD bless you and keep you;
The LORD make His face shine upon you,
And be gracious to you;
The LORD lift up His countenance upon you,
And give you peace.

—NUMBERS 6:24–26

Day 4

The Lord will bless you with a revelation of Himself, thereby giving you clear signposts that point out the right road on which you are to walk. Your integrity and uprightness will protect you because our hope is in God.

Day 5

God's faithfulness, mercy, and loving-kindness shall be with you, and in His name shall your strength be exalted. Great power and prosperity shall be conferred upon you as you grow in the grace of spiritual strength, knowledge, and understanding of our Lord and Savior Jesus Christ.

SCRIPTURE READING

But My faithfulness and My mercy shall be
   with him,
And in My name his horn shall be exalted....
He shall cry to Me, "You are my Father,
My God, and the rock of my salvation."
            —PSALM 89:24, 26

Day 6

The Lord our God will help you maintain sound and godly wisdom and discretion today and every day. They are success to you, keeping you safe from defeat and disaster. They will keep you from stumbling off the godly trail.

Day 7

The Lord is giving you understanding and a heart to be just and fair in everything you do. You are a leader in your generation. Like the horizons for breadth and the ocean for depth, the understanding of a good leader is broad and deep.

SCRIPTURE READING

Do not withhold Your tender mercies from
    me, O LORD;
Let Your lovingkindness and Your truth con-
    tinually preserve me....
Be pleased, O LORD, to deliver me;
O LORD, make haste to help me!

                  —PSALM 40:11, 13

Day 8

The Lord is looking at you through eyes of mercy and forgiveness, through eyes of everlasting love and kindness. Let His loving-kindness and truth preserve you continually.

Day 9

The Holy Spirit is leading you to the Most High God who is your place of safety and protection. He is our God, and He will cover you with His feathers, and under His wings you can hide. His truth is your shield and protection.

SCRIPTURE READING

He who dwells in the secret place of the Most
    High
Shall abide under the shadow of the
    Almighty.
I will say of the LORD, "He is my refuge and
    my fortress;
My God, in Him I will trust."

—PSALM 91:1–2

Day 10

When troubles rise like a flood, they will not reach you. God is your hiding place. He protects you from troubles and fills you with songs of salvation. God is your protection and strength. Because He always helps in times of trouble, you will not be afraid even if the earth shakes, the mountains fall into the sea, or the oceans roar and foam.

Day 11

My child, I pray for you to understand that the ways of God are without fault; the Lord's words are pure. He is a shield to all that trust Him. God is your protection, and He makes your way free from fault. I ask the Lord to make you like a deer that does not stumble, to help you stand on the steep mountains.

SCRIPTURE READING

As for God, His way is perfect;
The word of the LORD is proven;
He is a shield to all who trust in Him.
　　　　　　　　　—2 SAMUEL 22:31

Day 12

My precious one, you were born to serve God all the days of your life. God is strong, and He helps you walk in His ways. Your help comes from the Lord who made heaven and earth. He will not let you be defeated; He never sleeps. The Lord guards you. He is the shade that protects you from all dangers; He guards your life as you come and go, both now and forever.

Day 13

The Father is drawing you to Himself. When you are older, you will call upon the name of the Lord and receive eternal life, salvation. The all-powerful Lord is blessing you with knowledge and understanding that you may honor Him. He is blessing you with the experiential knowledge of unconditional love.

SCRIPTURE READING

And this is the will of Him who sent Me, that everyone who sees the Son and believes in Him may have everlasting life; and I will raise him up at the last day.

—JOHN 6:40

Day 14

My precious child, the Lord helps you develop your abilities so that you can assume your responsibilities in a way that reflects His nature in all of creation. When you are older, you will believe in the Son of God, Jesus. He will give you eternal life and raise you on the last day. This is what He wants for you, and I praise Him for your complete salvation.

Day 15

Jesus anoints your ears to hear what He says because you believe in the Father who sent Him, and you shall have eternal life. You shall listen to the voice of our God. You will know Him and follow Him. He will give you eternal life, and you shall never perish. No one can snatch you out of the Father's hand.

SCRIPTURE READING

For by grace you have been saved through faith, and that not of yourselves; it is the gift of God, not of works, lest anyone should boast.
—EPHESIANS 2:8–9

Day 16

Our Father sent Jesus who came as light into the world so that you will believe and not live in darkness. When you call on the name of the Lord, you will be saved. It is by grace that we are saved through faith. It is the gift of God, not by works, so that no one can boast.

Day 17

God sent the Holy Spirit to be your Friend and Counselor so that you always have Someone with you. This Friend is the Spirit of Truth. You shall know Him, and He will stay with you and even be in you!

SCRIPTURE READING

And I will pray the Father, and He will give you another Helper, that He may abide with you forever—the Spirit of truth, whom the world cannot receive, because it neither sees Him nor knows Him; but you know Him, for He dwells with you and will be in you.

—JOHN 14:16–17

Day 18

God is holding your head and shoulders above all those who would try to pull you down. You are headed for His place to offer anthems that will raise the roof! You have a heart and mind to trust God all the time. You can tell Him all of your problems because He is your protection.

Day 19

Here I am before the Lord with you, my little one, eyes open, drinking in His strength and glory. In His generous love you are really living at last! Your lips brim praises like fountains. You will bless Him every time you take a breath; your arms wave like banners of praise to God.

SCRIPTURE READING

Because Your lovingkindness is better than
    life,
My lips shall praise You.
Thus I will bless You while I live;
I will lift up my hands in Your name.

—PSALM 63:3–4

Day 20

God always remains close to you. He is your divine protection. You will tell your generation about all that God has done, and He will bless you with clean hands and a pure heart. The Lord God, who saves, will declare your righteousness. You are following Him in obedience to your parents.

Day 21

Our Lord has blessed you with His love, and you will glory in His holy name. He has given you a heart to seek Him and rejoice. He is your strength. Because you seek His face, He gives you the grace to trust Him more and more. I dedicate you to God, and He gives you a joyful spirit and gladness of heart.

SCRIPTURE READING

I will hear what God the LORD will speak,
For He will speak peace
To His people and to His saints;
But let them not turn back to folly.
Surely His salvation is near to those who fear
    Him,
That glory may dwell in our land.
—PSALM 85:8–9

Day 22

You are a wonderful gift from God. As you grow older, you will listen to Him. God has ordered peace for you, and you will worship Him. He will keep you from foolishness and save you, for you shall respect the Lord. Goodness and mercy shall follow you all the days of your life.

Day 23

I bless you and pray that as you grow older, you will desire to seek first the kingdom of God and His righteousness. All things pertaining to life and godliness will be added unto you. The Father blessed you by choosing you before the foundation of the world. I believe that as you grow up, you will love the Lord your God with all your heart, with all your soul, and with all your strength.

SCRIPTURE READING

You shall love the LORD your God with all your heart, with all your soul, and with all your strength.

—DEUTERONOMY 6:5

Day 24

God's Word is a lamp to your feet and a light for your path. His plans will be your plans, and God will enable you to live them. I bless you, my little one. May God always protect you with salvation-armor, hold you up with a firm hand, and caress you with His gentle ways. I thank God for hearing us when we pray.

Day 25

I am grateful when we laugh and play together. I declare that every bone in your body is laughing and singing, "God, there's no one like You." The Lord picks you up and puts you on your feet when you are feeling down. He will protect you from those who oppose you. His outstretched arms protect you, and under them, you are perfectly safe. He fends off all harm so that it does not come near you.

SCRIPTURE READING

And my soul shall be joyful in the LORD;
It shall rejoice in His salvation.
All my bones shall say,
"LORD, who is like You,
Delivering the poor from him who is too
 strong for him,
Yes, the poor and the needy from him who
 plunders him?"

—PSALM 35:9–10

Day 26

The Lord is watching over you—the Lord is your shade at His right hand. He is your Guardian, right at your side to protect you. I thank God for keeping you safe. He will keep you out of the clutches of the wicked and protect you from vicious people. God, our Lord, is a strong Savior.

Day 27

Little one, *I* bless you. Even while you are here in my protection, I pray that God will go before you and rescue you from the grip of unwholesome men and women so that you can live life God's way.

SCRIPTURE READING

But let all those rejoice who put their trust in
    You;
Let them ever shout for joy, because You
    defend them;
Let those also who love Your name
Be joyful in You.

—PSALM 5:11

Day 28

I thank God for welcoming you with open arms when you run to Him for cover. May He spread His protection over you that He may rejoice in you because you love His name. I thank God for blessing you, keeping watch over you, and keeping you out of trouble. I am assured that He will be there when you run to Him.

Day 29

Bless you, my child. May you be enthroned in God's presence forever. I ask God, our Father, to appoint His love and faithfulness to protect you. I ask the Lord to guard your life, for I am devoted to Him. He is our God. I ask Him to save you, my beloved child, for I trust in Him.

SCRIPTURE READING

I will abide in Your tabernacle forever;
I will trust in the shelter of Your wings....
For You, O God, have heard my vows;
You have given me the heritage of those who
    fear Your name.

—PSALM 61:4–5

Created for His Pleasure

Your Child's Destiny

As a child of God, your young child has a glorious calling to fellowship with Christ (1 Cor. 1:9), to holiness (1 Thess. 4:7), to a prize (Phil. 3:14), to liberty (Gal. 5:13), to peace (1 Cor. 7:15), to glory and virtue (2 Pet. 1:3), to the eternal glory of Christ (2 Thess. 2:14), and to eternal life (1 Tim. 6:12). Certainly this is not a complete list, but it is clear that because of Jesus Christ your child is very special and has an eternal destiny. She is a beauty and wonder to behold in the eyes of God. His love for her is so great that God the Father gave His only begotten Son for her, so that she would spend eternity with Him. He is her Father God. He is her eternal heavenly Father. "As a father pities his children, so the LORD pities those who fear Him. For He knows our frame; He remembers that we are dust" (Ps. 103:13–14).

Jesus Christ died on the cross so that your child could have life and life more abundantly. John recorded these words of Jesus: "I have come that they may have life, and that they may have it more abundantly" (John 10:10). He gave the gift of Himself to her. The apostle Paul wrote, "But God demonstrates His own love toward us, in that while we were still sinners, Christ died for us" (Rom. 5:8). Because of Him, she can live forevermore. Because of Him, she can have joy unspeakable. Because of Him, her life on earth can have eternal significance. The blessings and treasures in Christ Jesus that are laid up for your child cannot be counted by man.

Your child is an integral part of God's overall plan for mankind. She is called to be a vessel through which truth and love will flow from God to other people. As you pray for and bless your child each day, keep in mind that God has a specific call upon her life. He has given her individual talents and gifts for her to use as she fulfills God's plan for her life. She is called according to the purposes of God to be part of a chosen people, a royal priesthood, a holy nation, a people belonging to God (1 Pet. 2:9). She is also set apart to fulfill a specific purpose as a part of the larger body of Christ. "For we are His workmanship, created in Christ Jesus for good works, which God prepared beforehand that we should walk in them" (Eph. 2:10).

There is much to celebrate, much reason to rejoice. As God's plans for your own life unfold, you will also be watching the Lord's workmanship and creation blossom into what He created your child to do. As your child gives God pleasure in the days ahead, your own joy will become full. Your dedication to your child gives God great pleasure. Each day your expressions of faith in God, your love for Him, and your tender care of your child are all purposes that He created you to do. "For it is God who works in you both to will and to do for His good pleasure" (Phil. 2:13).

Day 1

Sweet precious one, I bless you. God made you a whole being; He formed you. I praise God because He made you in an amazing and wonderful way. What He has done is wonderful. The Father has wonderful plans for you.

SCRIPTURE READING

My frame was not hidden from You,
When I was made in secret,
And skillfully wrought in the lowest parts of
    the earth.
Your eyes saw my substance, being yet
    unformed.
And in Your book they all were written,
The days fashioned for me,
When as yet there were none of them.
—PSALM 139:15–16

Day 2

The Lord has examined you. He knows all about you. He knows when you sit down and when you get up. He knows your thoughts before you think them. He knows where you will go and where you will lie down. He knows thoroughly everything you will do. May He keep you under the protection of His wings.

Day 3

Even before you say a word, the Lord already knows it. He is all around you—in front and in back—and He has put His hand on you. If you climb to the sky, He is there! If you fly on morning's wings to the far, western horizon, He will find you in a minute—He will already be there waiting! You can know that He even sees you in the dark! At night you are immersed in the light!

SCRIPTURE READING

You have hedged me behind and before,
And laid Your hand upon me....
Where can I go from Your Spirit?
Or where can I flee from Your presence?
—PSALM 139:5, 7

Day 4

When you were being formed, God placed eternity in your heart. I pray and believe that you will do what is good. May you do what is right to other people and love being kind to others. Always obey God. Your real help in every situation comes from the Lord. His blessing will clothe you throughout your entire life.

Day 5

By Christ Jesus, God created you to join in His work, the good work He has planned for you to do. My child, you were created for His good pleasure. May He continually create in you a new and clean heart that is filled with pure thoughts and right desires.

SCRIPTURE READING

Who created the heavens,
Who is God,
Who formed the earth and made it,
Who has established it,
Who did not create it in vain,
Who formed it to be inhabited:
I am the LORD, and there is no other.

—ISAIAH 45:18

Day 6

May God bless you with a heart of faithfulness. May you understand that we are children of the same father, Abraham, all created by the same God. May He teach you what it means to be faithful to others and to keep the covenant of our spiritual fathers.

Day 7

I bless you, little one. I pray that you will be happy from the inside out and from the outside in—for you are firmly formed and loved. I bring you before the Lord. You are the work of His hands, of absolute truth and justice, faithful and right. May you always stand steadfast and remain established in Christ Jesus forever and ever.

SCRIPTURE READING

The works of His hands are verity and justice;
All His precepts are sure.
They stand fast forever and ever,
And are done in truth and uprightness.
—PSALM 111:7–8

Day 8

I bless you, little one. With His very own hands God formed and fashioned you. Now I ask Him to breathe His wisdom over you so you can understand Him. He created you. He formed you. You do not have to be afraid because He has saved you. He has called you by name, and you are His.

Day 9

The Lord said, "Bring to me all the people who are mine, whom I made for my glory, whom I formed and made." I now bring you before the Lord on this wondrous day, asking Him to bless you to follow paths of righteousness.

SCRIPTURE READING

Everyone who is called by My name,
Whom I have created for My glory;
I have formed him, yes, I have made him....
This people I have formed for Myself;
They shall declare My praise.

—ISAIAH 43:7, 21

Day 10

Little one, He who made you, who formed you in the womb, and who will help you, says, "Do not be afraid." I bless you. Before God formed you in the womb He knew you, and before you were born He set you apart. He appointed you to tell about the wonderful acts of God. You were created for His pleasure.

Day 11

In the name of Jesus, I speak His Word and bless you, our little one. It was God who made you. You are His! We are His people and the sheep of His pasture. Praise the name of the Lord! I thank God for pouring His Spirit upon you, my child, and His blessing upon our descendants. They shall spring up among the grass, as willows or poplars by the watercourses.

SCRIPTURE READING

What is man that You are mindful of him...?
You have crowned him with glory and honor.
You have made him to have dominion over
    the works of Your hands;
You have put all things under his feet.
—PSALM 8:4–6

Day 12

I thank God for giving me this precious gift. I am encouraged because you are important to God, and He takes care of you. You belong to God. He put human beings in charge of everything that He made, and He put all things under their control. May He teach you to walk in this God-given authority and glorify His name.

Day 13

Little one, the Lord has assigned you His portion and His cup; He has made your lot secure. May God make known to you the path of life and fill you with joy in His presence and with eternal pleasures at His right hand.

SCRIPTURE READING

O LORD, You are the portion of my inheri-
tance and my cup;
You maintain my lot....
You will show me the path of life;
In Your presence is fullness of joy;
At Your right hand are pleasures forevermore.
—PSALM 16:5, 11

Day 14

Just as the Father took Jesus out of the womb, so He brought you forth out of the womb. God knows you, our little one. When you call on the Lord, He will answer you and make you bold and stouthearted. I declare that He shall be your God, and you will not be far from Him.

Day 15

I thank our God for you because you are breathtaking! Body and soul, you are marvelously made! God made you inside and out. I rejoice in the works of His hands. God knows every bone in your body. He knows exactly how you were made, bit by bit, how you were sculpted from nothing into something.

SCRIPTURE READING

And we know that all things work together for good to those who love God, to those who are the called according to His purpose.
—ROMANS 8:28

Day 16

In all things God works for the good of those who love Him, who have been called according to His purpose. I thank God that He created you for His good pleasure. Nothing shall separate you from the love of Christ. Because of the way that Jesus our Master has embraced you, little one, absolutely nothing can come between you and God's love.

Day 17

I pray that God's love will be at the center of your heart and that you will never fake it. I pray for God to give you the courage to run from evil and hold on for dear life to good. May you be a good friend who loves deeply and delights in honoring others.

SCRIPTURE READING

Do you not know that your body is the temple of the Holy Spirit who is in you, whom you have from God, and you are not your own? For you were bought at a price; therefore glorify God in your body and in your spirit, which are God's.

—1 CORINTHIANS 6:19–20

Day 18

I believe that your body was made for God-given and God-modeled love, for "becoming one" with another who loves Him. I pray that you will always respect your body as a sacred place, the place of the Holy Spirit. You were bought with a price; therefore I pray that you will glorify God in your body and in your spirit, which are God's.

Day 19

I pray that you will be an imitator of God and walk in love. I ask the Lord to teach you to love others. I ask the Lord to teach you to walk as a child of light, for the fruit of the Spirit is in all goodness, righteousness, and truth.

SCRIPTURE READING

See then that you walk circumspectly, not as fools but as wise, redeeming the time, because the days are evil.

—EPHESIANS 5:15–16

Day 20

I pray that God will teach you wisdom so that you may understand what the will of the Lord is. I also ask that honesty and integrity will be your virtue and protection. May you be granted with a calm, collected, and circumspect attitude about life that you might obtain salvation through our Lord Jesus Christ.

Day 21

I pray that you will be strong, courageous, and firm throughout your life, and that God will be with you. May God give you a desire to do good, to be rich in good works, and to be liberal, generous-hearted, and ready to share with others.

SCRIPTURE READING

Let them do good, that they be rich in good works, ready to give, willing to share, storing up for themselves a good foundation for the time to come, that they may lay hold on eternal life.

—1 TIMOTHY 6:18–19

Day 22

May the God of our Lord Jesus Christ, Father of glory, give you the spirit of wisdom and revelation in the knowledge of Him. I ask that God would grant to you, according to the riches of His glory, to be strengthened with might through His Spirit in your inner man.

Day 23

May Christ dwell in your heart through faith. I ask the Father to teach you how to be rooted and grounded in love, and to be able to comprehend, with all the saints, what is the width, length, depth, and height of the love of Christ, which passes knowledge, so that you may be filled with all the fullness of God.

SCRIPTURE READING

Restore to me the joy of Your salvation,
And uphold me by Your generous Spirit.
—PSALM 51:12

Day 24

I ask God to make known to you the path of life and to fill you with joy in His presence and with eternal pleasures at His right hand. May the Lord grant you the joy of His salvation and grant you a willing spirit to sustain you.

Day 25

Jesus loves you even as the Father loves Him. May you ever remain in His love. I thank Jesus that you are well and whole. He has given you the gift of peace.

SCRIPTURE READING

Therefore, as the elect of God, holy and beloved, put on tender mercies, kindness, humility, meekness, longsuffering; bearing with one another, and forgiving one another.
—COLOSSIANS 3:12

Day 26

May God grant you a daily walk of humility and gentleness. I pray for Him to help you to be patient, bearing with others in love. I thank God for choosing you for this new life of love. May you dress in the wardrobe He picked out for you: compassion, kindness, humility, quiet strength, and discipline.

Day 27

May the Lord impart to you a strong desire to follow close behind Him, where you will be protected by His strong right arm. I ask God to help me teach you responsibility, for He has said that you must take responsibility for doing the creative best you can with your own life.

SCRIPTURE READING

We should no longer be children, tossed to and fro and carried about with every wind of doctrine...but, speaking the truth in love, may grow up in all things into Him who is the head—Christ.

—EPHESIANS 4:14–15

Day 28

May God instill a desire in you to lovingly follow the truth at all times—that you may speak truly, deal truly, live truly—and so become more and more in every way like Christ who is the head of His body, the church.

Day 29

May God grant you a glad heart and a joyful spirit. The Holy Spirit will teach you to pray unceasingly; no matter what happens, may you always be thankful. I pray that every detail in your life will be done in the name of the Master, Jesus, and that you will thank Father God every step of the way.

SCRIPTURE READING

Rejoice always, pray without ceasing, in everything give thanks; for this is the will of God in Christ Jesus for you.

—1 THESSALONIANS 5:16–18

Day 30

Since such a great cloud of witnesses surrounds you, I pray for God to teach you to throw off everything that hinders and the sin that so easily entangles. Little one, run with perseverance the race marked out for you.

$\mathcal{D}ay$ 31

$\mathcal{M}y$ *prayer is* that you will discover that God's Word is better than a diamond, better than a diamond set between emeralds. I pray that you will grow in the grace and knowledge of our Lord and Savior Jesus Christ. We give Him glory both now and forever! Amen.

SCRIPTURE READING

Grow in the grace and knowledge of our Lord and Savior Jesus Christ.

—2 PETER 3:18

Everything Is Beautiful

*N*eed
to *P*ray

Because there are so many commands in the Bible for us to pray, it is impossible to be obedient to God if we do not have a life of prayer. Among the numerous scriptures that command us to pray are, "Pray without ceasing, in everything give thanks" (1 Thess. 5:17–18), and "Watch and pray" (Matt. 26:41).

Prayer is the gateway to blessing. "Ask, and it will be given to you; seek, and you will find; knock, and it will be opened to you. For everyone who asks receives, and he who seeks finds, and to him who knocks it will be opened" (Matt. 7:7–8).

Prayer is needed for power, for intimacy with God, and for protection against the power of the devil and temptations of this world. It brings fullness of joy and brings us into the realm of the heavenlies. When you pray, you can be confident that God will reveal to you more about His nature, give you revelation of truth that will guide you in your daily life, and work on your behalf in sovereign and divine ways.

When you pray according to the Word of God, you are praying in accordance with the will of God, and He will hear you. Since the prayers and blessings in this book have been taken from the Word of God, you can be confident that you are praying according to the will of God for your child. "Now this is the confidence that we have in Him, that if we ask anything according to His will, He hears us. And if we know that He hears us, whatever we ask, we know that we have the petitions that we have asked of Him" (1 John 5:14–15).

As you pray for your child, believe that those things that you are asking for in accordance with the Word of God will come to pass. You may not see the fulfillment of those prayers and words right now, but your faith will grow as you speak and hear the truth of God's Word. Just as the world was framed by the Word of God, your child's life will also be framed by His Word as you pray and speak words of blessing accordingly. "Now faith is the substance of things hoped for, the evidence of things not seen. For by it the elders obtained a good testimony. By faith we understand that the worlds were framed by the word of God, so that the things which are seen were not made of things which are visible" (Heb. 11:1–3).

Praying for and blessing your child according to the Word and will of God, thereby pointing him to Jesus, is the greatest gift you could give him.

Day 1

I thank God for you, our beautiful child. I pray for God to enable you to see the wonder of your birth and your value to this family. He has made everything beautiful in its time.

SCRIPTURE READING

He has made everything beautiful in its time. Also He has put eternity in their hearts, except that no one can find out the work that God does from beginning to end.

—ECCLESIASTES 3:11

Day 2

By His Spirit, God will help us learn to recognize the power of His beauty in us so that we may do well. I am thankful to Him for His blessings, which make our lives rich today. You, my child, shall be a loving worker in Christ Jesus. The work of His hands is beautiful in His sight.

Day 3

My child, you have been made to live in beautiful dwelling places. I ask God to keep you safe, and I accept my responsibility for you. I ask God to send angels ahead of you to guard your way and bring you back to the place that He has prepared for you.

SCRIPTURE READING

> But whoever listens to me will dwell safely,
> And will be secure, without fear of evil.
> —PROVERBS 1:33

Day 4

On this day I purpose to train you in His ways, and you will not depart from them. God created you to be a beautiful person with self-respect, and you will learn to be respectful of others. I purpose not to exasperate you, my child, and I pray that you will receive instruction in the Lord.

Day 5

God has a time for everything and a season for every activity under heaven. I pray that God will help set our priorities in order so that I am encouraged and can say that the Lord is our Helper.

SCRIPTURE READING

For the people shall dwell in Zion at
    Jerusalem;
You shall weep no more.
He will be very gracious to you at the sound
    of your cry;
When He hears it, He will answer you.
                                    —ISAIAH 30:19

Day 6

I thank the Lord that He is with us. There is a time for emotional expression in our lives, and I acknowledge His intervention with joy. I thank God for blessing you, my child, with a good sense of humor.

Day 7

A cheerful heart is a good medicine. I thank our heavenly Father that His Word abides in you this day so that you may respect others. May your words always be used to cheer up others.

SCRIPTURE READING

A merry heart does good, like medicine,
But a broken spirit dries the bones.

—PROVERBS 17:22

Day 8

On this day, I lift up praises to the Lord. May His praises continually be in your mouth, even at this time. It is beautiful to be full of God. May you recognize that there is a time for everything.

Day 9

God sent the Holy Spirit to help you be organized in your life. When you don't know what to do, ask God, our Father, for wisdom; He will cause wisdom to enter your heart so that knowledge will be pleasant to your soul. God always keeps His Word because He is watching over it.

SCRIPTURE READING

When wisdom enters your heart,
And knowledge is pleasant to your soul,
Discretion will preserve you;
Understanding will keep you.
—PROVERBS 2:10–11

Day 10

I rejoice in His salvation. May you have much time to reflect on Jesus and to be secure that you are saved along with this household. Young child, keep these thoughts near your heart, and toss away all fear.

Day 11

I have great confidence that you will be all that God desires. He has prepared a way of safety, and He will protect you. He is your confidence. May we always rejoice in the beauty of our time together. He is our help.

SCRIPTURE READING

In returning and rest you shall be saved;
In quietness and confidence shall be your
strength.

—ISAIAH 30:15

Day 12

See how good our God is! Be blessed, young child. Trust and take your refuge in Him. Reverence the Lord; worship Him. You will have no want if you truly revere and worship Him with a godly fear. I will train you in His ways.

Day 13

I uproot any unforgiveness that has planted itself in our spirits today and declare that it will not have any effect on you, my child. I forgive those who have sinned against me; therefore, God shall forgive me. I hold this as God's promise. May God give you a heart that is quick to forgive.

SCRIPTURE READING

To them [His saints] God willed to make known what are the riches of the glory of this mystery among the Gentiles: which is Christ in you, the hope of glory.

—COLOSSIANS 1:27

Day 14

I petition God for the salvation of all those whom He has ordered for you to reach with the gospel during your lifetime. His salvation makes men's spirits beautiful in His time. I ask for repentance in their hearts so that they may be forgiven and come to the knowledge of God.

Day 15

God has put great love in our hearts for one another. He has perfected and made us complete in Jesus. I purpose to walk in love individually and as a family so that we can bless others.

SCRIPTURE READING

How beautiful are the feet of those who
preach the gospel of peace,
Who bring glad tidings of good things!
—ROMANS 10:15

Day 16

You will be in places to receive the good news of the gospel. You will respect those who come to present His Word. You will worship the Lord in the splendor of His holiness. May He open your eyes to see the beauty of His time.

Day 17

The teachings of our Lord have fallen like rain and His words like dew. Dear one, you are the tender plant that receives the rain. God is giving you understanding so that you may meditate on His beautiful wonders.

SCRIPTURE READING

I have not hidden Your righteousness within
my heart;
I have declared Your faithfulness and Your
salvation;
I have not concealed Your lovingkindness and
Your truth
From the great assembly.

—PSALM 40:10

Day 18

I thank God for His loving-kindness that He brought to our family this day. He keeps His Word, and you are privileged to be included in His covenant. I will speak of His faithfulness and salvation to you, my child, and He will reveal His love and truth to you.

Day 19

Lie down in peace this evening, dear child, because our dwelling place is secure. You can rest; you are secure in God. God has shielded you all day long. You can look about and rest in hope.

SCRIPTURE READING

In the fear of the LORD there is strong confi-
   dence,
And His children will have a place of refuge.
The fear of the LORD is a fountain of life,
To turn one away from the snares of death.
                                —PROVERBS 14:26–27

Day 20

My child, let's rejoice in the beauty of our God! He has made everything beautiful in its time. Bask in God's love, and see the beauty in His creation. Acknowledge His plan and purpose for mankind.

Day 21

God is at work to make you a man (or woman) of knowledge who uses words with restraint. He will help you remain even-tempered in your relations with others. I praise God that no deceit will be found in you.

SCRIPTURE READING

He who has knowledge spares his words,
And a man of understanding is of a calm
spirit.

—PROVERBS 17:27

Day 22

I thank God for the love He has poured out into our hearts by the Holy Spirit. I ask God to fill your heart with His love. You will love God with all your heart, with all your soul, and with all your mind. His love allows you to love others as you love yourself.

Day 23

I ask the Lord to teach you to love from a pure heart, from a good conscience, and from unfeigned faith. May God help you to live a life of unfeigned faith that He has imparted as a gift to you and to me.

SCRIPTURE READING

And these words which I command you today shall be in your heart. You shall teach them diligently to your children, and shall talk of them when you sit in your house, when you walk by the way, when you lie down, and when you rise up.

—DEUTERONOMY 6:6–7

Day 24

His Word is in our minds and hearts, and I purpose to teach them and impress them diligently upon your mind and heart, my child. I ask God to give you a hunger to know His Word. Together as a family, we will talk of His truth when we sit down or take a walk, when we lie down, and when we rise up.

Day 25

I thank God for granting consolation and joy to you, and for giving you an ornament of beauty, the oil of joy, and a garment of praise. I thank God that you shall be called an oak of righteousness (lofty, strong, and magnificent; distinguished for upright-ness, justice, and right standing with our God), the planting of the Lord, that He might be glorified.

Scripture Reading

The LORD has anointed Me...
To give them beauty for ashes,
The oil of joy for mourning,
The garment of praise for the spirit of
    heaviness;
That they may be called trees of
    righteousness,
The planting of the LORD, that He may be
    glorified.

—Isaiah 61:1, 3

Day 26

I thank God for causing your steps to be firm and steadfast, immovable, and always abounding in the work of the Lord. May God give you insight so that you will know and be continually aware that your labor in the Lord is not futile, never wasted, or to no purpose.

Day 27

Our beautiful little one, you belong to the household of faith, and you are God's true child according to a common faith. I bless you, my child, with grace, favor, spiritual blessing, and with a heart of peace from God the Father and the Lord Christ Jesus our Savior.

SCRIPTURE READING

The sun shall no longer be your light by day,
Nor for brightness shall the moon give light
    to you;
But the LORD will be to you an everlasting
    light,
And your God your glory.

—ISAIAH 60:19

Day 28

Little one, I speak God's Word over you and ask the Holy Spirit to always bring it to your remembrance. The Lord shall be to you an everlasting light in His glory and His beauty.

Day 29

The Holy Spirit will always be with you to help you walk righteously and speak uprightly. As you do this, your eyes will see the King in His beauty, and they will behold a land of wide distances that stretches afar.

SCRIPTURE READING

Give to the LORD, O families of the peoples,
Give to the LORD glory and strength.
Give to the LORD the glory due His name;
Bring an offering, and come into His courts.
—PSALM 96:7–8

Day 30

You will grow up and offer yourself willingly in the day of His power, in the beauty of holiness, and in holy array. When you are older, you will ascribe to Him glory and strength; you will give Him the glory due His name. You will bring an offering, come into His courts, and worship Him in the beauty of holiness.

Character
Building

The Power of Praise

Along with blessing our children, we can also bless the Lord. We can do this by recognizing His characteristics, His sovereignty, His loving-kindness, and His other attributes. An example of this can be found in Ephesians 1:3: "Blessed be the God and Father of our Lord Jesus Christ, who has blessed us with every spiritual blessing in the heavenly places in Christ." Just think of the magnitude of the blessing that is being spoken of here. It is important to note that when this scripture says "has blessed us," it is referring to you and your young child. If you are living in Christ Jesus, the two of you are part of the word *us* in this scripture. Blessed be God, for you and your young child have been blessed with all spiritual blessings in heavenly places in Christ. Consider just how many blessings and words of faith you can speak over your child as you come into agreement with the Word of God!

Praises to God will fill your home and your heart in such a way that there is no room for despair and feelings of defeat. Instead of keeping our eyes fixed on our troubles and daily tasks, we turn our attention to praising our almighty King. He rules and reigns over every situation and over every task at hand. As we praise the Lord, joy springs forth in our hearts, and our strength is renewed. It may not be chains of iron that are broken; instead, it may be chains of worry or affliction. But just as the prayers and praises broke the chains of Paul and Silas in Acts 16, praying to God and praising Him will break our chains today, thereby enabling us to be a greater blessing to our child and to other people.

This book is a guidepost of daily blessings, prayers, and expressions of praise and thanksgiving. While I encourage you to refer to and use this book each day, I also suggest that you fill your life and home with praises to God all day long: "Speaking to one another in psalms and hymns and spiritual songs, singing and making melody in your heart to the Lord" (Eph. 5:19). Let your child hear you singing songs of praise, lifting up your voice to the Lord in thanksgiving. Let her see the smile on your face and the gleam in your eye that come from lifting your voice in praise to Him. "For the LORD is good; His mercy is everlasting, and His truth endures to all generations" (Ps. 100:5). Yes, His truth endures to you and to the generations after you and after your child. His truth calls us to come to Him with thanksgiving and praise to bless His holy name.

Day 1

I dedicate you for the work of the ministry, asking God to anoint you as a leader among men. You are a child sent to lead others to Jesus. I rejoice, knowing that the earth shall be full of the knowledge of the Lord as the waters cover the sea.

Scripture Reading

He has shown you, O man, what is good;
And what does the LORD require of you
But to do justly,
To love mercy,
And to walk humbly with your God?

—Micah 6:8

Day 2

May God open the eyes of your understanding so that you may know that God is sovereign over all. I ask God to give you a reverence for the life of God in others so that you may esteem and delight in them.

Day 3

The Father God will cause you to be strong and courageous! You shall not be afraid! God is your light, and He makes any darkness bright.

SCRIPTURE READING

Without counsel, plans go awry,
But in the multitude of counselors they are
established.

—PROVERBS 15:22

Day 4

The Father goes before you, and He will bless you with wise advisers. His plans for you will not fail. He will cause you to become a man (or woman) of understanding, drawing out the purposes of His heart for your future.

Day 5

May God bless you to apply your heart to instruction and your ears to words of knowledge. I pray that you will have a heart to commit to the Lord whatever you do, and then your plans will succeed.

SCRIPTURE READING

Commit your works to the LORD,
And your thoughts will be established.
—PROVERBS 16:3

Day 6

I pray that you will know skill, godly wisdom, and instruction so that you may discern and comprehend the words of understanding and insight. I pray that you will receive instruction in dealing wisely, in the discipline of wise thoughtfulness, righteousness, justice, and integrity.

Day 7

In your youth, may God give to you prudence, knowledge, discretion, and discernment. May God grant you wisdom that you may hear and increase in learning. As a person of understanding, may you acquire skill and attend to sound counsel so that your course will be steered by God.

SCRIPTURE READING

But whoever listens to me will dwell safely,
And will be secure, without fear of evil.
—PROVERBS 1:33

Day 8

I pray that you will hearken to wisdom so that you may dwell securely, in confident trust and in quietness without fear or dread of evil.

Day 9

God is creating a desire in your heart and mind for insight. You will raise your voice for understanding, seek for wisdom as silver, and search for skillful and godly wisdom as for hidden treasures.

SCRIPTURE READING

Yes, if you cry out for discernment,
And lift up your voice for understanding,
If you seek her as silver,
And search for her as for hidden treasures;
Then you will understand the fear of the
   LORD,
And find the knowledge of God.
—PROVERBS 2:3–5

Day 10

May God grant you an understanding of the reverent and worshipful fear of the Lord so that you may find the knowledge of our omniscient God.

Day 11

God is giving you a desire to follow the steps of the godly and stay on the right path. He will cause you to be a man (or woman) of integrity, blameless and complete in God's sight, and you shall enjoy fullness of life.

Scripture Reading

So you may walk in the way of goodness,
And keep to the paths of righteousness.
For the upright will dwell in the land,
And the blameless will remain in it.
—Proverbs 2:20–21

Day 12

I pray that you will trust God from the bottom of your heart. May you always listen for God's voice in everything you do and everywhere you go. I trust the Lord to keep you on track.

Day 13

May you honor the Lord with your wealth, with the first fruits of all of your crops. I pray that you will never tire of loyalty and kindness, and ask that you hold these virtues tightly and write them deep within your heart.

SCRIPTURE READING

Honor the LORD with your possessions,
And with the firstfruits of all your increase;
So your barns will be filled with plenty,
And your vats will overflow with new wine.
—PROVERBS 3:9–10

Day 14

I ask God to keep you free of conceit. Instead, may you ever trust and reverence the Lord, and may you turn your back on evil. May the Lord bless you to know right from wrong, and may you have good judgment and common sense.

Day 15

I pray that your goals will be to know and do right, and to have common sense. May you not let them slip away, for they will fill you with living energy and bring you honor and respect. May you always acknowledge that the Lord is your confidence and that He shall keep your foot from being caught.

SCRIPTURE READING

Keep sound wisdom and discretion;
So they will be life to your soul
And grace to your neck.
Then you will walk safely in your way,
And your foot will not stumble.

—PROVERBS 3:21–23

Day 16

I receive God's promise on your behalf. His Holy Spirit shall not leave you, and you shall want the good and hate the wrong.

Day 17

The Lord is imparting to you a desire to do good to those who deserve it when it is in your power to act. I thank the Father for blessing you with a heart of integrity so that you may fulfill your obligations as a good citizen. I have asked Him to instill in you a desire to pay your taxes, pay your bills, and respect your leaders.

SCRIPTURE READING

Render therefore to all their due: taxes to whom taxes are due, customs to whom customs, fear to whom fear, honor to whom honor.

—ROMANS 13:7

Day 18

I praise God believing that every time you get the chance, you will work for the benefit of all, starting with the people closest to you in the community of faith.

Day 19

I pray that you will hear the instruction of your earthly father and your heavenly Father, and that you will pay attention in order to gain and to know intelligent discernment, comprehension, and interpretation of spiritual matters.

SCRIPTURE READING

Hear, my children, the instruction of a father,
And give attention to know understanding....
"Let your heart retain my words;
Keep my commands, and live."
—PROVERBS 4:1, 4

Day 20

I pray to the Lord God of hosts that your heart will hold fast the words of truth and that you will keep His commandments and live.

89

Day 21

It is the Father's good pleasure to open the eyes of your understanding so that you may know Him in a personal way. You will become intimately acquainted with Him. You will understand Him, appreciate and heed His instructions, and cherish Him.

SCRIPTURE READING

> As for you, my son Solomon, know the God of your father, and serve Him with a loyal heart and with a willing mind....If you seek Him, He will be found by you.
>
> —1 CHRONICLES 28:9

Day 22

I pray that you will serve God with a blameless heart and a willing mind. Find comfort in knowing that He searches all hearts and minds and understands all the wanderings of the thoughts. May His will be done in your life on earth as it is in heaven.

Day 23

I ask God to give you comprehensive insight into His ways and purposes and to lead you in paths of uprightness. When you walk, your steps shall not be hampered; when you run, you shall not stumble.

SCRIPTURE READING

I have taught you in the way of wisdom;
I have led you in right paths.
When you walk, your steps will not be
    hindered,
And when you run, you will not stumble.
          —PROVERBS 4:11–12

Day 24

Because I have asked the Father in the name of Jesus, He is granting you the ability to concentrate and pay attention to His words so that you may consent and submit to His sayings. It is my prayer that His words will not depart from your sight and that you will keep them in the center of your heart.

Day 25

I ask the Lord to grant you the ability to pay attention to our wisdom and listen well to our words of insight so that you may maintain discretion and your lips preserve knowledge.

SCRIPTURE READING

My son, pay attention to my wisdom;
Lend your ear to my understanding,
That you may preserve discretion,
And your lips may keep knowledge.
—PROVERBS 5:1–2

Day 26

Little one, our ways are directly before His eyes, and He, who would have us to live soberly, chastely, and godly, carefully weighs all men's goings.

Day 27

I ask the Holy Spirit to help you to follow your father's good advice. May you never wander off from your mother's teachings. I pray that you will wrap yourself in good advice and sound teaching from head to foot, wearing them like a scarf around your neck.

SCRIPTURE READING

My son, keep your father's command,
And do not forsake the law of your mother....
When you roam, they will lead you;
When you sleep, they will keep you;
And when you awake, they will speak with you.
—PROVERBS 6:20, 22

Day 28

I pray that where you walk, good advice and sound teachings will guide you; whenever you rest, they will guard you; and when you wake up, they will tell you what lies ahead.

Day 29

I affirm that you will keep His commandments and live, and keep His teaching as the apple (the pupil) of your eye. The Holy Spirit will help you bind them on your fingers and write them on the tablet of your heart.

SCRIPTURE READING

For my mouth will speak truth;
Wickedness is an abomination to my lips.
All the words of my mouth are with righ-
   teousness;
Nothing crooked or perverse is in them.

—PROVERBS 8:7–8

Day 30

I ask God to help me to be a good example to you. Then you will speak excellent and princely things, and the opening of your lips shall be for right things. I pray that all the words of your mouth will be righteous, upright, and in right standing with God.

Day 31

God is giving you an open mind so that you will recognize truth. He is instructing me so that I might teach you that skillful and godly wisdom is better than rubies or pearls, and all the other things that you may desire are not to be compared to it.

SCRIPTURE READING

Receive my instruction...
For wisdom is better than rubies,
And all things one may desire cannot be com-
pared with her.
—PROVERBS 8:10–11

The Lord Keeps Watch

Give Thanks

Praising God and thanking Him are certainly closely related, but when we express thanksgiving to God, we are often thanking Him for specific blessings from which we have benefited.

So often the Lord blesses us abundantly, yet we don't approach Him with an attitude of thankfulness before we begin to ask Him for something else. However, if we stop to meditate on the grace, mercy, and love of the majestic Ruler we serve, we begin to understand how His very nature calls us to enter into His presence with thanksgiving and praise. Thankfulness will be ignited in us when we begin to consider the wonder and splendor of the mighty King whose throne is heaven and whose footstool is earth. This glorious King, our mighty God who communes with us, is not only the Ruler of the universe, but He is also concerned about everything that concerns us. He even knows the number of hairs that are on our heads. Is it any wonder that the Scriptures give us the pattern of how we should approach our King as described in Psalm 100:4? "Enter into His gates with thanksgiving, and into His courts with praise. Be thankful to Him, and bless His name."

Philippians 4:6 tells us that our requests in prayer must be accompanied by thanksgiving. "But in everything by prayer and supplication, with thanksgiving, let your requests be made known to God." Further confirmation of this is given in Colossians 4:2: "Continue earnestly in prayer, being vigilant in it with thanksgiving." So not only are we to pray and be thankful, but we are to be devoted to it.

We have so much for which to be thankful. In fact, everything wonderful around us comes from Him. The gift of eternal life through our Lord and Savior Jesus Christ comes from Him. The beauties we behold, the laughter, the warmth, the comfort we find in family and friends, the sorrows that shape our character, the bounty of His creation—all these and so much more come from Him. Yes, even the child you hold close to your heart comes from Him. Everything, absolutely everything, good comes from Him. "Every good gift and every perfect gift is from above, and comes down from the Father of lights, with whom there is no variation or shadow of turning" (James 1:17).

So give God thanks. Thank Him for what He has already done. Dedicate yourself and your child wholly to Him, and thank Him for the promises He is about to fulfill in your lives.

Day 1

I pray that our Father God will always shield you, our precious baby, on all sides and give you courage. I am thankful that God always hears our prayers.

SCRIPTURE READING

Be still, and know that I am God.
—PSALM 46:10

Day 2

I believe that you, our little one, are marked for God's kingdom. I know that He will bless you, for surely He blesses the righteous. He will surround you with His favor as with a shield.

Day 3

The Lord is your fort where you can enter and be safe. He is a rugged mountain where you can hide. He is your Savior, a rock where none can reach you and a tower of safety.

SCRIPTURE READING

The LORD is my rock and my fortress and my
    deliverer;
My God, my strength, in whom I will trust;
My shield and the horn of my salvation, my
    stronghold.

—PSALM 18:2

Day 4

May Father God give you the desires of your heart as you delight yourself in Him.

101

Day 5

I thank the Lord for this day that He has made. Little one, the angels are at His command, and He will command His angels concerning you, to guard you in all your ways.

SCRIPTURE READING

Cause me to hear Your lovingkindness in the
    morning,
For in You do I trust;
Cause me to know the way in which I should
    walk,
For I lift up my soul to You.

—PSALM 143:8

Day 6

May Father God wake you each morning with the sound of His loving voice; then you will go to sleep each night trusting in Him. He will point out the road you must travel, and you shall lie down and sleep in peace and wake up safely, for the Lord is watching over you.

Day 7

I thank God that you will lie down and sleep in peace, for the Lord alone makes you dwell in safety. Because He watches over Israel, and He neither slumbers nor sleeps, He will watch over you.

SCRIPTURE READING

Behold, He who keeps Israel
Shall neither slumber nor sleep.
The LORD is your keeper;
The LORD is your shade at your right hand
The sun shall not strike you by day,
Nor the moon by night.

—PSALM 121:4–5

Day 8

When you lie down, you will not be afraid; when you lie down, you will sleep in peace.

Day 9

I thank God that you will keep our commands, and you will not forsake the law of your mother. Wherever you walk, they will guide you; whenever you rest, they will guard you; when you wake up, they will tell you what's next.

SCRIPTURE READING

When you roam, they will lead you;
When you sleep, they will keep you;
And when you awake, they will speak with you.
—PROVERBS 6:22

Day 10

The Holy Spirit is present to anoint your ears to hear the words of Jesus and give you the desire to put them into practice. You will be like the wise man (or woman) who builds his (or her) house on the rock. Even though the floods may come and the winds may blow, your house will stand.

Day 11

It is the Father's good pleasure to reveal to you just as He did to Simon Peter that Jesus is the Christ, the Messiah, the Son of the living God.

SCRIPTURE READING

Then Jesus said to them, "Come after Me, and I will make you become fishers of men." And immediately they left their nets and followed Him.

—MARK 1:17–18

Day 12

The grace of God is imparted to you, and you will follow the Lord always. When you call, He will answer, and He will make you a fisherman for the souls of men!

Day 13

As you mature, you will learn to love the Lord God with all your passion, prayer, intelligence, and energy. Because He first loved you, you will love others as you love yourself.

SCRIPTURE READING

You shall love the LORD your God with all your heart, with all your soul, with all your mind, and with all your strength....You shall love your neighbor as yourself.

—MARK 12:30–31

Day 14

As you grow in the grace and knowledge of Jesus Christ, you will learn how necessary it is for you to pray consistently and never quit.

Day 15

I thank God for giving you the capacity to receive the revealed knowledge that Jesus is the Way, the Truth, and the Life, and you can come to the Father at anytime through Him.

SCRIPTURE READING

I am the vine, you are the branches. He who abides in Me, and I in him, bears much fruit; for without Me you can do nothing.

—JOHN 15:5

Day 16

May the Holy Spirit give you the understanding that Jesus is the Vine and you are the branch. If you are in Him, you will bear much fruit.

Day 17

I pray that when the time arrives, you will repent and be baptized in the name of Jesus Christ for the remission of sins, and you will receive the gift of the Holy Spirit.

SCRIPTURE READING

> Then Peter said to them, "Repent, and let every one of you be baptized in the name of Jesus Christ for the remission of sins; and you shall receive the gift of the Holy Spirit."
> —ACTS 2:38

Day 18

I pray that when you are an adult living in your own home, you and your household will believe on the Lord Jesus Christ and be saved.

Day 19

You are God's offspring. In Him, you live, move, and have your being. May you be most proud to proclaim this extraordinary message of God's powerful plan to rescue everyone who trusts Him, starting with Jews and then to everyone else!

SCRIPTURE READING

For I am not ashamed of the gospel of Christ, for it is the power of God to salvation for everyone who believes, for the Jew first and also for the Greek.

—ROMANS 1:16

Day 20

May your love always be real. I pray that you will hate what is evil, and hold on to what is good.

Day 21

I have asked our Father to shed His love abroad in your heart, and I pray that your love will always be real. You will learn to hate what is evil and hold on to what is good.

SCRIPTURE READING

[Love] bears all things, believes all things, hopes all things, endures all things. Love never fails.

—1 CORINTHIANS 13:7–8

Day 22

I pray that you will walk in the kind of love that bears all things, believes all things, hopes all things, and endures all things. This kind of love will never fail.

Day 23

I pray that you will keep your eyes open for spiritual danger, stand true to the Lord, act like a godly man (or woman), and be strong. In all that you do, may you do it with kindness and love.

SCRIPTURE READING

Watch, stand fast in the faith, be brave, be strong. Let all that you do be done with love.
—1 CORINTHIANS 16:13–14

Day 24

I bless you to speak truth at all times. The Lord will set a guard over your mouth and keep watch over the door of your lips.

Day 25

When you receive Jesus as your Lord, you will become a brand-new person inside. You will not be the same any longer. A new life begins!

SCRIPTURE READING

> Therefore, if anyone is in Christ, he is a new creation; old things have passed away; behold, all things have become new.
> —2 CORINTHIANS 5:17

Day 26

Before the Father, I bless you, our son (or daughter) with grace and peace from God our Father and the Lord Jesus Christ. I thank Jesus for giving Himself for our sins to rescue you from the present evil age, according to the will of our God and Father.

Day 27

When we ask, while believing, God gives His children divine energy. May you ever be strengthened in your innermost being by the Holy Spirit. Then you will never get tired of doing good, for at the right time you will harvest a good crop if you don't quit or give up.

SCRIPTURE READING

And let us not grow weary while doing good, for in due season we shall reap if we do not lose heart.

—GALATIANS 6:9

Day 28

God our Father will help you keep your eyes focused and clear so that you can see exactly what the Lord is calling you to do. Because the Holy Spirit is present to direct you, you will grasp the immensity of the glorious way of life He has for His children.

Day 29

May you be strong in the Lord and in His mighty power and have the desire to put on the full armor of God so that you can take your stand against the devil's schemes.

SCRIPTURE READING

Put on the whole armor of God, that you may be able to stand against the wiles of the devil. For we do not wrestle against flesh and blood, but against principalities, against powers, against the rulers of the darkness of this age, against spiritual hosts of wickedness in the heavenly places.

—EPHESIANS 6:11–13

Day 30

I thank God for His peace that garrisons and mounts a guard over your heart and mind through Christ Jesus as you prepare to go to sleep.

Peace That Passes Understanding

The Tongue Must Be Bridled

Now is the time to choose the type of environment in which your child will grow. Will he grow up hearing praises and blessings, or will he have to cringe at the sound of cursing? There are many forms of cursing, all of which are destructive and hurtful. Daily we are faced with choices to either bless or curse, to bridle our tongue or to open the gateway of destruction. Like David, the prayer of hearts must be, "Let the words of my mouth and the meditation of my heart be acceptable in Your sight, O LORD, my strength and my Redeemer" (Ps. 19:14).

Our prayer each day should also be, "Set a guard, O LORD, over my mouth; keep watch over the door of my lips" (Ps. 141:3). Imagine a home where a child is never called an ugly name and never hears gossip, complaining, arguing, hurtful accusations, words of doubt, malice, guile, self-condemnation, lying, cheating, selfishness, pride, or filthiness! You may ask yourself, "Is this possible?" The answer to

116

that question lies in the scripture, "Let no corrupt word proceed out of your mouth, but what is good for necessary edification, that it may impart grace to the hearers" (Eph. 4:29).

Out of the same mouth can come both blessings and cursing, but this should not be the case. If we have decided to bless our children in accordance with the Word of God, then it is important for us to be consistent. We must not bless them one minute and curse them in anger the next. We must not praise God, only to then turn around and speak accusations and complaints against Him or members of the family of believers. "With it [the tongue] we bless our God and Father, and with it we curse men, who have been made in the similitude of God. Out of the same mouth proceed blessing and cursing. My brethren, these things ought not to be so" (James 3:9–10).

The principle of sowing and reaping applies to the words we speak. Though it will take self-discipline, if we seek God's wisdom and rely on Him to help us maintain an environment of blessings and praises to God, the harvest will be great. "And let us not grow weary while doing good, for in due season we shall reap if we do not lose heart. Therefore, as we have opportunity, let us do good to all, especially to those who are of the household of faith" (Gal. 6:9–10).

If we rejoice in all things, even during times of difficulty, then our gentleness will be evident to everyone around us, including our own children. Rather than relying on our own strength and becoming anxious, we can do the very opposite of

117

that by presenting our requests to God through prayer and thanksgiving. The end result will be that the peace of God, which transcends all understanding, will guard our hearts and our minds in Christ Jesus (Phil. 4:4–7). To bridle the tongue we must also bridle the mind. What we choose to think about will guide our actions, reactions, and words. In fact, Philippians 4:8 tells us exactly what to think about: "Finally, brethren, whatever things are true, whatever things are noble, whatever things are just, whatever things are pure, whatever things are lovely, whatever things are of good report, if there is any virtue and if there is anything praiseworthy—meditate on these things."

Praise God for the wonderful child He has given you. God has wonderful plans for him and for you. "But as it is written: 'Eye has not seen, nor ear heard, nor have entered into the heart of man the things which God has prepared for those who love Him.' But God has revealed them to us through His Spirit" (1 Cor. 2:9–10). Ask God for wisdom for you to understand what He has prepared for you and your child in Christ Jesus. To the natural mind, His plans are incomprehensible, but by His Spirit the Lord will give you understanding and bold confidence as you put on the mind of Christ.

Day 1

I bless you, precious one whom God has sent to me. I thank God for sending you a special Friend, the Holy Spirit, who will make everything plain to you. I thank Jesus for keeping you well and whole. He has given you a beautiful parting gift: peace.

SCRIPTURE READING

But the Helper, the Holy Spirit, whom the Father will send in My name, He will teach you all things, and bring to your remembrance all things that I said to you. Peace I leave with you, My peace I give to you.

—JOHN 14:26–27

Day 2

The Lord bless you and keep you, little one; the Lord make His face shine upon you and be gracious to you; the Lord turn His face toward you and give you peace.

Day 3

Praise God for His faithfulness! He is granting you the will to listen carefully to all He is saying—for He speaks peace to you. I pray that you will always choose to do the right thing.

SCRIPTURE READING

Mercy and truth have met together;
Righteousness and peace have kissed.
Truth shall spring out of the earth,
And righteousness shall look down from
    heaven.

—PSALM 85:10–11

Day 4

His Word declares that mercy and truth have met together. Righteousness and peace have kissed! Truth rises from the earth, and righteousness smiles down from heaven. I thank the Lord for His blessings that He will pour down on you.

Day 5

I confess that Jesus is Lord of our family. I ask Him to open your eyes that you may know Jesus as "Wonderful," "Counselor," "The Mighty God," "The Everlasting Father," "The Prince of Peace."

SCRIPTURE READING

The work of righteousness will be peace,
And the effect of righteousness, quietness and
    assurance forever.

—ISAIAH 32:17

Day 6

I thank the Father that we are His people, and you, our precious child, will live in a peaceful dwelling place, in a secure home, in an undisturbed place of rest.

Day 7

Before our heavenly Father, I bless you. I pray that you will not fear or be dismayed as you fulfill your destiny. You and your descendants will have peace and security, and no one will make you afraid, for God is with you.

SCRIPTURE READING

Therefore do not fear, O My servant Jacob,
　　says the LORD....
For behold, I will save you from afar,
And your seed from the land of their captivity.
　　　　　　　　　　　　—JEREMIAH 30:10

Day 8

I enter into the covenant of peace God made with His children, an everlasting pact. I thank God for blessing you and future generations. The Lord God has made His home among us. He is our God, and we are His people.

Day 9

Through the heartfelt mercies of our God, God's sunrise will break in upon you, shining on you even if you are in the darkness. Then God's sunrise will show you the way, one foot at a time, down the path of peace.

SCRIPTURE READING

Peace I leave with you, My peace I give to you; not as the world gives do I give to you. Let not your heart be troubled, neither let it be afraid.

—JOHN 14:27

Day 10

I thank God for His peace that He left with us—the peace He gave to you. I pray that you will not let your heart be troubled and that you will not be afraid as you pursue the more abundant life.

Day 11

In the name of Jesus, I loose thoughts of fretting and anxiety from your mind. I bind you—spirit, soul, and body—to God's peace, which transcends all understanding. This peace will guard your heart and mind in Christ Jesus.

SCRIPTURE READING

I will give you the keys of the kingdom of heaven, and whatever you bind on earth will be bound in heaven, and whatever you loose on earth will be loosed in heaven.

—MATTHEW 16:19

Day 12

Jesus gave us the keys of the kingdom of heaven. Whatever we bind on earth will be bound in heaven, and whatever we loose on earth will be loosed in heaven. I bind your spirit, soul, and body to the peace of God.

Day 13

Note to parents: The following prayer is one that I heard my father pray each night just before bedtime. He continued to pray this for his family throughout his lifetime. This prayer was my consolation in times of distress and delivered me from many fears.

I bow my knee to the Father of our Lord Jesus Christ. We can lie down in peace and sleep, knowing that the angel of the Lord encamps around about our home and keeps us safe.

SCRIPTURE READING

The angel of the LORD encamps all
   around those who fear Him,
And delivers them.

—PSALM 34:7

Day 14

When you lie down, you will not be afraid; when you lie down, your sleep will be sweet.

Day 15

The Lord Almighty declared that in this place He would give peace. We receive this promise for our household and our future generations. I pray for the Lord to keep you safe even when you are alone. You will lie down in peace and sleep.

SCRIPTURE READING

These things I have spoken to you, that in Me you may have peace. In the world you will have tribulation; but be of good cheer, I have overcome the world.

—JOHN 16:33

Day 16

I pray that you will hear, understand, and trust the words of Jesus; then you will be unshakable and assured, deeply at peace. Even though you will experience difficulties in this godless world, you will take heart because Jesus conquered the world!

Day 17

God's peace has been given to you, and you will experience His peace, which is far more wonderful than the human mind can understand. His peace will keep your thoughts and heart quiet and at rest as you learn to trust in Christ Jesus our Lord.

SCRIPTURE READING

For He Himself is our peace, who has made both one, and has broken down the middle wall of separation.

—EPHESIANS 2:14

Day 18

I thank God that He continues to bless me each day, giving me the wisdom to teach you how to get along with others. God is giving you His wisdom that is gentle and reasonable, overflowing with mercy and blessings. It is not hot one day and cold the next, but consistent every day. He is creating in you a desire to be like Jesus.

Day 19

May you run away from infantile indulgence as you develop spiritually, mentally, emotionally, and physically. I believe that you will run after mature righteousness—faith, love, and peace—joining those who are in honest and serious prayer before God.

SCRIPTURE READING

Flee also youthful lusts; but pursue righteousness, faith, love, peace with those who call on the Lord out of a pure heart.

—2 TIMOTHY 2:22

Day 20

I purpose to bless you with peacemaking techniques through instruction and practice. You will be blessed when you can show people how to cooperate instead of compete or fight. That's when you will discover who you really are and find your place in God's family.

Day 21

I pray that you will be a blameless man (or woman) and walk uprightly, for your future will be one of peace.

SCRIPTURE READING

Mark the blameless man, and observe the
    upright;
For the future of that man is peace.

—PSALM 37:37

Day 22

I pray for the Lord to help me remember and teach you to stir up goodness, peace, and joy from the Holy Spirit. May you pursue the things that make for peace and the things by which one may edify another.

Day 23

I thank the Father for blessing you. You will live in joy and peace. The mountains and hills, the trees of the field—all the world around you—will rejoice.

SCRIPTURE READING

All your children shall be taught by the
    LORD,
And great shall be the peace of your children.
                                —ISAIAH 54:13

Day 24

He sent His Holy Spirit to teach you and to lead you into all truth. I pray that you shall be taught by the Lord. Great shall be your peace.

Day 25

I pray that you will grow in spiritual strength and become more intimately acquainted with our Lord and Savior Jesus Christ. To Him be all glory and splendid honor, both now and forevermore.

SCRIPTURE READING

Grow in the grace and knowledge of our Lord and Savior Jesus Christ. To Him be the glory both now and forever. Amen.

—2 PETER 3:18

Day 26

In stressful moments, may the Holy Spirit remind you of the words of our Lord, "It's all right. Don't be afraid!"

Day 27

God knows the refinement that you will need. I pray that you will submit to the constant ministry of transformation by the Holy Spirit. You will learn right from wrong as you practice doing right. Nothing will please me more than to find you walking in Truth, just as I have been commanded by Him to do.

SCRIPTURE READING

Do not be conformed to this world, but be transformed by the renewing of your mind, that you may prove what is that good and acceptable and perfect will of God.

—ROMANS 12:2

Day 28

I pray that you will not copy the behavior and customs of this world, but be a new and different person with a fresh newness in all you do and think. Then you will learn from your own experience how His ways will really satisfy you.

Day 29

In the name of Jesus, I bind your plans for the future to His plans for you. May God give you a clear vision for the future. The vision is yet for an appointed time. Although it tarries, you will wait for it because it will surely come.

SCRIPTURE READING

> For I know the thoughts that I think toward you, says the LORD, thoughts of peace and not of evil, to give you a future and a hope.
> —JEREMIAH 29:11

Day 30

I pray and believe that as the deer pants for streams of water, so shall your soul pant for God. I pray that your soul will thirst for the living God. I ask the Holy Spirit to show you where to go and meet with God.

Day 31

I pray that you will walk blamelessly before God. A wonderful future lies ahead for the good, blameless, upright man or woman. There is a happy ending for you.

SCRIPTURE READING

You shall be blameless before the LORD your God.

—DEUTERONOMY 18:13

Learn to Listen and Pray

*P*ray, *L*isten, and *R*est

In the still moments of the morning and evening, hold your young child in your arms, pray, and listen. What is the Lord saying to you today? Is He revealing His plans for you and your child? Do you sense His presence in the stillness?

As you thank the Lord, praise Him, bless Him, and speak blessings over your child, don't forget to also spend quiet time with the Lord. It is often in those moments that He will reveal Himself to you in deeper and broader ways. He may also surprise you with instruction and guidance on situations that seemed to be impossible just moments ago. "Call to Me, and I will answer you, and show you great and mighty things, which you do not know" (Jer. 33:3).

If we do not purpose to set aside quiet time with the Lord, it is easy to get caught up in the hustle and bustle and duties of life. Oftentimes, we then begin to work in our own strength because we have not been relying on Him for His strength. Then we often become consumed with worries and distracted by the natural world. If we disregard our spiritual needs, His voice will be further and further drowned out by the cares of this life. Bit by bit our peace can be replaced by confusion, a short temper, feelings of being overwhelmed, and exhaustion.

It may seem that having a young child in the house makes it impossible to spend time with the Lord, but moving from duty to duty without spending any quiet time with the Lord will only make matters worse. You were called to peace, not constant hardship. Yes, there is labor and trouble in this life, but Jesus sent the Holy Spirit to comfort and to guide you. Do not let the workload or problems of the day rule your day; instead, look for moments to rest in Him. "Let the peace of God rule in your hearts, to which also you were called in one body; and be thankful" (Col. 3:15).

Jesus wants to give you rest. He wants you to lay your burdens at His feet and rest from your own labors. Many times we just make life too hard. If we would only be transparent and take our burdens to the Lord, our loads would be so much lighter. Jesus said, "Come to Me, all you who labor and are heavy laden, and I will give you rest. Take My yoke upon you and learn from Me, for I am gentle and lowly in heart, and you will find rest for your souls. For My yoke is easy and My burden is light" (Matt. 11:28–30).

There is a place of rest that we obtain when we lay our burdens at His feet and our concerns in His hands. We can also rest in the fact that we have a High Priest who understands our weaknesses. He is ready to help us. He knows the temptations and struggles we face. In Him, we will find the help we need. We may think we know what we need, but time and again we discover that His thoughts and ways are above our own. His answer is always exactly what we needed. "Let us therefore come boldly to the throne of grace, that we may obtain mercy and find grace to help in time of need" (Heb. 4:16).

Day 1

I bless you and pray that you will fully obey the Lord your God and carefully follow all His commandments. The Lord your God will set you high above all the nations on earth.

SCRIPTURE READING

You are of God, little children, and have overcome them, because He who is in you is greater than he who is in the world.

—1 JOHN 4:4

Day 2

God has redeemed us. Greater is He that is in us than he that is in the world.

Day 3

I thank God for His Word that will sustain us. He will never allow the (consistently) righteous to be moved (made to slip, fall, or fail). Our little child, the Lord cares for you affectionately and cares about you watchfully.

SCRIPTURE READING

Cast your burden on the LORD,
And He shall sustain you;
He shall never permit the righteous to be
   moved.

—PSALM 55:22

Day 4

I bless you and pray that you will always listen to the Lord. You will be blessed when you listen to the voice of the Good Shepherd. I pledge myself to help you watch daily at His doors and to wait at His doorway. You will find life and receive favor from the Lord.

Day 5

I thank the Father for the good work He has begun in you. I am confident that He will carry it on to completion until the day of Christ Jesus.

SCRIPTURE READING

Being confident of this very thing, that He who has begun a good work in you will complete it until the day of Jesus Christ.

—PHILIPPIANS 1:6

Day 6

Now I pray that our God will hear the prayers and petitions of His servants. I pause and listen for His Spirit. May His peace surround us. I thank God that you are learning to listen to God.

Day 7

Beloved child of the Lord, I give thanks always to God for you, because God chose you from the beginning for salvation. You were chosen out of the world, and you are a special child to God and to me.

SCRIPTURE READING

Do not be afraid of sudden terror,
Nor of trouble from the wicked when it
  comes;
For the LORD will be your confidence,
And will keep your foot from being caught.
—PROVERBS 3:25–26

Day 8

For the Lord shall be your confidence, firm and strong; He shall keep your foot from being caught in a trap or some hidden danger. Listen to the words of peace from the Lord.

Day 9

The Father has blessed you with ears to hear when the Lord stands at the door and knocks. When you hear His voice and open the door, He will come in and eat with you, and you with Him. Awake to righteousness. Listen and enjoy the company of the Lord.

SCRIPTURE READING

Behold, I stand at the door and knock. If anyone hears My voice and opens the door, I will come in to him and dine with him, and he with Me.

—REVELATION 3:20

Day 10

May God anoint your ears to always listen to the Lord, for He will never forsake you. Your inheritance is that His good Spirit will instruct you.

Day 11

God has wonderful plans for you, and He is giving you the ability to learn to be content and at peace. You will acquire the life skills that will make you a whole person, complete in Jesus.

SCRIPTURE READING

Blessed be the God and Father of our Lord Jesus Christ, who according to His abundant mercy has begotten us again to a living hope through the resurrection of Jesus Christ from the dead, to an inheritance incorruptible and undefiled and that does not fade away, reserved in heaven for you.

—1 PETER 1:3–4

Day 12

Praised (honored, blessed) be the God and Father of our Lord Jesus Christ (the Messiah)! You, our little baby, have been born to receive an ever-living hope through the resurrection of Jesus. You are born into an inheritance that is beyond the reach of destruction.

Day 13

May the Lord guide you and reveal His will to you. You will pray to Him, and He will hear you, and you will fulfill your vows. What you decide on will be done, and light will shine on your ways.

SCRIPTURE READING

Deliver me, O LORD, from my enemies;
In You I take shelter.
Teach me to do Your will,
For You are my God;
Your Spirit is good.
Lead me in the land of uprightness.

—PSALM 143:9–10

Day 14

I bless you, my child, that you might take a firm stand and a tight grip on what you are taught about God. May Jesus Himself and God our Father, who reached out in love, invigorate you and enliven you.

Day 15

God calls you righteous. The prayer of the upright pleases Him. Listen, and God will bring you peace. Listen, and hear what Jesus said. He says that if you believe in Him, the works that He does, you will do even greater. You have a wonderful future prepared for you.

SCRIPTURE READING

Therefore I say to you, whatever things you ask when you pray, believe that you receive them, and you will have them.

—MARK 11:24

Day 16

Whatever you ask for according to the will of God, believe that you have received it, and it will be yours. Thank you for listening to the Lord.

Day 17

As you grow up, devote yourself to prayer, being watchful and thankful. Let the peace of Christ rule in your heart, for you are a member of one body, which is called to peace.

SCRIPTURE READING

Let the peace of God rule in your hearts, to which also you were called in one body; and be thankful.

—COLOSSIANS 3:15

Day 18

Be still and wait for the Lord God, and you will be glad and rejoice in His salvation.

Day 19

Sweet one, we will go into your room and pray to our Father who is in the secret place; your Father who sees in secret will reward you.

SCRIPTURE READING

We give thanks to the God and Father of our Lord Jesus Christ, praying always for you.
—COLOSSIANS 1:3

Day 20

I give thanks to God the Father of our Lord Jesus Christ, praying always for you. You shall bring forth good fruit and know the grace of God in truth and love in the Spirit.

Day 21

This day may you be strengthened with all might, according to God's glorious power, unto all patience and longsuffering with joyfulness. I give thanks to our heavenly Father and come near to call upon Him in truth. He will fulfill the desire of those who fear Him; He also will hear their cry and save them.

SCRIPTURE READING

The LORD is near to all who call upon Him,
To all who call upon Him in truth.
He will fulfill the desire of those who fear
    Him;
He also will hear their cry and save them.
                          —PSALM 145:18–19

Day 22

Little one, I bless you and pray for you continually. I will watch over you with prayer and thanksgiving. Even as I teach you of the mystery of Christ, I will continue in prayer for you. I will labor fervently for you in prayers, that you may stand perfect and complete in all the will of God.

Day 23

Little one, I desire to be an example to you and to pray always without ceasing. When you are older you will pray and give thanks in everything, for this is the will of God in Christ Jesus concerning you.

SCRIPTURE READING

> But we are bound to give thanks to God always for you, brethren beloved by the Lord, because God from the beginning chose you for salvation through sanctification by the Spirit and belief in the truth.
>
> —2 THESSALONIANS 2:13

Day 24

Thanks be to God for you, beloved of the Lord. From the beginning God chose you to salvation through sanctification of the Spirit and belief of the truth. God loves you and has given you everlasting consolation and good hope through grace.

Day 25

Today, *I shall* pray to God for you, and He will delight in you. The Lord our God is in our midst; the Mighty One saves. He rejoices over you with gladness. He quiets you with His love, and He rejoices over you with singing.

SCRIPTURE READING

Therefore I will look to the LORD;
I will wait for the God of my salvation;
My God will hear me.

—MICAH 7:7

Day 26

This morning, *I* pray to the Lord for He is good, and He gives abundant mercy to all those who call upon Him. When we call Him, He will answer.

151

Day 27

There will be times when you lack wisdom. Ask God, and He will liberally give His wisdom to you so that you will know what to do. Do not waiver, but ask in faith. Every good and perfect gift is from above and comes down from the Father of lights, with whom is no variableness, neither shadow of turning.

SCRIPTURE READING

Every good gift and every perfect gift is from above, and comes down from the Father of lights, with whom there is no variation or shadow of turning.

—JAMES 1:17

Day 28

Little one, if you are ever in trouble, you should pray. If you are happy, sing songs of praise. Little one, I entreat you to listen to God, for He will give you His peace.

Day 29

Our little one, what a God we have! The Father of Jesus has given us a brand-new life so that we have everything to live for, including a future in heaven, which starts now. God is keeping careful watch over you. The day is coming when you will have it all.

SCRIPTURE READING

But without faith it is impossible to please Him, for he who comes to God must believe that He is, and that He is a rewarder of those who diligently seek Him.

—HEBREWS 11:6

Day 30

Little one, the God of all grace, who has called us into His eternal glory by Christ Jesus, will make you perfect, establish, strengthen, and settle you. To God be glory and dominion forever and ever. Amen.

Day 31

As you learn and grow, little one, I bless you with God's Word, which says that if you call to Him, He will answer you and tell you great and unsearchable things you do not know.

Scripture Reading

Call to Me, and I will answer you, and show you great and mighty things, which you do not know.

—Jeremiah 33:3

The Good Shepherd Carries His Lambs

$\mathscr{H}$is
$\mathscr{B}$lessings

$\mathscr{N}o$ book $\mathit{written}$ by man could possibly number the blessings of God or measure His goodness. Each day can be a new discovery of learning more about Him. Our revelation of His character can be increased each day. In fact, we are to receive the fresh manna, the fresh bread, of the Word of God each day.

In Psalm 119:105, we are told that God's Word will light the path we are to follow: "Your word is a lamp to my feet and a light to my path." As you speak these blessings over your child and read the recommended scriptures, you will learn and be reminded of the abundance of God's goodness, mercy, and blessings. It is my prayer that your understanding of His power and your knowledge of Him will increase with each passing day and that you will pass the truth of God's Word on to your children and your children's children.

Just how expansive are the blessings that the Lord has stored up for you and your child? The answer is simple: every good thing is available to you in Christ Jesus if you walk uprightly before Him. "The LORD God is a sun and shield; the LORD will give grace and glory; no good thing will He withhold from those who walk uprightly" (Ps. 84:11).

Through knowledge of Him, you will be given everything you need—not just some of the things you need, but all. By His power, He is able and wants to provide for all your spiritual and physical needs. "His divine power has given to us all things that pertain to life and godliness, through the knowledge of Him who called us by glory and virtue" (2 Pet. 1:3).

As you bless your child each day, remember that God is a rewarder of them who diligently seek Him. You and your child are part of the family of God and are therefore inheritors of all things in Christ Jesus. You are partakers of an inheritance that will never fade away. Old things become new in Christ Jesus, the Author and the Finisher of our faith, "who according to His abundant mercy has begotten us again to a living hope through the resurrection of Jesus Christ from the dead, to an inheritance incorruptible and undefiled and that does not fade away, reserved in heaven for you, who are kept by the power of God through faith for salvation ready to be revealed in the last time" (1 Pet. 1:3–5).

When you go with your child before the Father in a time of a need, you can go boldly before the throne of grace, knowing that He will answer and that His Word will come to pass.

Day 1

Jesus is the Good Shepherd, and He tends His flock well. He gathers the lambs in His arms and carries them close to His heart. He will gently lead you, my little one.

SCRIPTURE READING

He will feed His flock like a shepherd;
He will gather the lambs with His arm,
And carry them in His bosom,
And gently lead those who are with young.
—ISAIAH 40:11

Day 2

I pray that you will put God in charge of your work so that what you have planned will take place.

Day 3

God has given each of us the ability to do certain things well. Therefore, if God has given you the ability to prophesy, then I bless you to prophesy whenever you can—as often as your faith is strong enough to receive a message from God.

SCRIPTURE READING

Having then gifts differing according to the grace that is given to us, let us use them: if prophecy, let us prophesy in proportion to our faith; or ministry, let us use it in our ministering.

—ROMANS 12:6–7

Day 4

If your gift is that of serving others, may you serve them well. If you are a teacher, I believe that you will do a good job of teaching. If you are a preacher, may God see to it that your sermons are strong and helpful.

Day 5

I continue to pray for your divine destiny. If God gives you money, I pray that you will be generous in helping others with it. If God gives you ability and puts you in charge of the work of others, I pray that you will take the responsibility seriously. I believe that you will always offer comfort and Christian cheer to the sorrowful.

Scripture Reading

…he who teaches, in teaching; he who exhorts, in exhortation; he who gives, with liberality; he who leads, with diligence; he who shows mercy, with cheerfulness.

—Romans 12:7–8

Day 6

I confess that the Lord is your Shepherd, and you will have everything you need! As you sleep tonight, God will let you rest in the meadow grass and lead you beside the quiet streams. He will give you new strength and help you do what honors Him most.

Day 7

I pray and believe that only goodness, mercy, and unfailing love shall follow you all the days of your life. Through the length of days the house of the Lord (and His presence) shall be your dwelling place.

SCRIPTURE READING

Show me Your ways, O LORD;
Teach me Your paths.
Lead me in Your truth and teach me,
For You are the God of my salvation.

—PSALM 25:4–5

Day 8

Little one, I bless you and pray that you will keep your eyes on Jesus, who both began and finished this race you're in. I pray for our heavenly Father to give you the desire to study how Jesus did it and to give you the courage to fulfill your destiny.

Day 9

I ask the Holy Spirit to teach you to trust God from the bottom of your heart. Then you will not try to figure out everything on your own.

SCRIPTURE READING

Trust in the LORD with all your heart,
And lean not on your own understanding;
In all your ways acknowledge Him,
And He shall direct your paths.
—PROVERBS 3:5–6

Day 10

God is a safe place for you to hide, and He is ready to help when you need Him. You can stand fearless at the cliff-edge of doom and courageous in a sea storm and earthquake, before the rush and roar of oceans or in the tremors that shift mountains. I thank God for fighting for you and surrounding you with armies of angels to protect you.

Day 11

We are praying that God will cause you to be steadfast and immovable so you will always abound in the work of the Lord.

SCRIPTURE READING

Therefore, my beloved brethren, be steadfast, immovable, always abounding in the work of the Lord, knowing that your labor is not in vain in the Lord.

—1 CORINTHIANS 15:58

Day 12

I ask the Holy Spirit to help me to teach you, my child, to pray at all times. May you ask God for anything in line with the Holy Spirit's wishes. You will learn how to plead with God and to keep praying earnestly for all Christians everywhere.

Day 13

No parent is more blessed than I am. I am so proud of you, and I believe that He who has shepherded me all my life will wonderfully bless you, my dear child.

SCRIPTURE READING

And he [Jacob] blessed Joseph, and said:

"God, before whom my fathers Abraham and
  Isaac walked,
The God who has fed me all my life long to
  this day,
The Angel who has redeemed me from all
  evil,
Bless the lads;
Let my name be named upon them,
And the name of my fathers Abraham and
  Isaac;
And let them grow into a multitude in the
  midst of the earth."

—GENESIS 48:15–16

Day 14

I thank God for protecting you. He will defend you, for He defends and blesses His chosen ones. He will lead you like a shepherd and carry you forever in His arms.

Day 15

The Shepherd of Israel, who leads Israel like a flock, is leading you, our little one. When you pray, God bends down His ear and listens. He plans to display His power and radiant glory to you. When we look at you, we shout, "Good job, God!"

SCRIPTURE READING

The LORD is their strength,
And He is the saving refuge of His anointed.
Save Your people,
And bless Your inheritance;
Shepherd them also,
And bear them up forever.

—PSALM 28:8–9

Day 16

Jesus is the Good Shepherd, and He knows His sheep. You were born for His glory, and you will know His voice because you belong to Him.

Day 17

The God of peace, who put you together, is providing you with everything you need to please Him, and He is making you into a man (or woman) who will give Him most pleasure, by means of the sacrifice of Jesus, the Messiah. You bring our Father much joy!

SCRIPTURE READING

Now may the God of peace who brought up our Lord Jesus from the dead, that great Shepherd of the sheep, through the blood of the everlasting covenant, make you complete in every good work to do His will, working in you what is well pleasing in His sight, through Jesus Christ, to whom be glory forever and ever. Amen.

—HEBREWS 13:20–21

Day 18

Because you come to me and listen, you are learning to revere the Lord. Reverence for the Lord is the beginning of wisdom.

Day 19

It comforts me to know that Jehovah God spreads His wings over you, even as an eagle overspreads her young. The eagle carries them upon her wings—as does the Lord carry His people!

SCRIPTURE READING

For this is God,
Our God forever and ever;
He will be our guide
Even to death.

—PSALM 48:14

Day 20

I acknowledge that our Father is this great God, and He is our God forever and ever. He will be your guide until you complete your life here on earth.

Day 21

You shall be like a tree planted by the rivers of water, that brings forth its fruit in its season, whose leaf shall not wither. Whatever you do shall prosper.

SCRIPTURE READING

A good man out of the good treasure of his heart brings forth good; and an evil man out of the evil treasure of his heart brings forth evil. For out of the abundance of the heart his mouth speaks.

—LUKE 6:45

Day 22

I ask our heavenly Father to give me wisdom to monitor what you hear and see. I believe that you will grow up to be a godly man (or woman), and out of the good treasure of your heart you will bring forth good. Out of the abundance of the heart your mouth will speak.

Day 23

I bless you and ask the Holy Spirit to counsel you, give you wisdom in the night, and tell you what to do. May you always think of the Lord; because He is so near, you will never need to stumble or fall.

SCRIPTURE READING

I will bless the LORD who has given me
    counsel;
My heart also instructs me in the night seasons.
I have set the LORD always before me;
Because He is at my right hand I shall not be
    moved.

—PSALM 16:7–8

Day 24

I pray that you will store up for yourself treasures in heaven, where moth and rust do not destroy and where thieves do not break in and steal. For where your treasure is, there your heart will be also.

Day 25

Little one, I pray that when the time comes for you to decide whom you will obey, you will have the courage to say, "But as for me and my family, we will serve the Lord."

SCRIPTURE READING

Seek the LORD while He may be found,
Call upon Him while He is near.

—ISAIAH 55:6

Day 26

Little one, I am confident that when you seek Him, you will find Him. You will call upon Him while He is near.

Day 27

Little one, may the Lord guide you continually, satisfy you with all good things, and keep you healthy, too. Then you will be like a well-watered garden, like an ever-flowing spring.

SCRIPTURE READING

I can do all things through Christ who strengthens me.

—PHILIPPIANS 4:13

Day 28

Little one, when you are faced with obstacles, may the Holy Spirit remind you of God's Word that says, "I can do all things through Christ who strengthens me."

*D*ay 29

I ask the Lord to give me the wisdom to teach you to wait upon Him. When you wait upon the Lord, He shall renew your strength. You shall mount up with wings like eagles; you shall run and not be weary; you shall walk and not faint.

SCRIPTURE READING

Then you shall delight yourself in the LORD;
And I will cause you to ride on the high hills
    of the earth,
And feed you with the heritage of Jacob your
    father.
The mouth of the LORD has spoken.

—ISAIAH 58:14

*D*ay 30

You are our delight, and when you delight in the Lord, He will cause you to ride on the high hills of the earth.

Be Not Afraid

His Word Will Come to Pass

The Word of the Lord will endure forever. It will not change. You can count on it. You can fully put your trust in His Truth. "But the word of the LORD endures forever" (1 Pet. 1:25). Because the blessings contained in this book are taken from the Word of God, you can be sure that your words will not fail. A great harvest of fruit will be produced by your words of blessing.

The Bible is not mere words of men. The Scriptures were fully inspired by God. The Word of God testifies of this very fact. Because the Scriptures are from God, they are fully reliable, infallible, and trustworthy. "All Scripture is given by inspiration of God" (2 Tim. 3:16). "For prophecy never came by the will of man, but holy men of God spoke as they were moved by the Holy Spirit" (2 Pet. 1:21).

The Bible tells us that Jesus Christ is the Word of God that was made flesh. Therefore, putting your trust in Jesus Christ is also putting your trust in the

174

Word of God. "And the Word became flesh and dwelt among us, and we beheld His glory, the glory as of the only begotten of the Father, full of grace and truth" (John 1:14).

Jesus Christ loved us so much that He gave Himself for us as an offering for our sins. Because of this, we are saved, healed, and delivered. God speaks His truth to us through His Son, Jesus Christ, the Word of God revealed in the flesh. "God, who at various times and in various ways spoke in time past to the fathers by the prophets, has in these last days spoken to us by His Son, whom He has appointed heir of all things, through whom also He made the worlds" (Heb. 1:1).

God is love, and the Word of God is the revelation of that love. His love and His Word will never fail. It will come to pass. Yes, we must obey Him and do our part, but we have the assurance that our steps will be ordered by Him if we follow His Word and His ways. When we accept Jesus as our Lord and Savior and serve Him and Him only, He is our beginning, our end, and everything in between.

God's Word will accomplish what He sent it forth to do in your life and in the life of your child. His purpose for which He sent it forth to do in your lives will surely come to pass. "For as the rain comes down, and the snow from heaven, and do not return there, but water the earth, and make it bring forth and bud, that it may give seed to the sower and bread to the eater, so shall My word be that goes forth from My mouth; it shall not return to Me void, but it shall accomplish what I please, and it shall prosper in the thing for which I sent it" (Isa. 55:10–11).

The Word of God is not just for the world in general. It is personal. It is for you and for your young child. His Word is a general truth, but it is also a personal truth to which you can cleave. Hide His Word in your heart, fully trusting in the fact His Word is for you and yours.

As you speak the Word of God over your child, let His will become your will. Believe for His absolute best for your child. Pray for His will to be done and His kingdom to come in the life of your little one and in your whole house. "So He said to them, 'When you pray, say: Our Father in heaven, hallowed be Your name. Your kingdom come. Your will be done on earth as it is in heaven'" (Luke 11:2).

Day 1

Little one, God is always present to watch over you. He cares for the birds that fly, and you are more valuable to Him than many birds. He will take care of you.

SCRIPTURE READING

Fear not, for I am with you;
Be not dismayed, for I am your God.
I will strengthen you,
Yes, I will help you,
I will uphold you with My righteous right
hand.

—ISAIAH 41:10

Day 2

Little one, you are blessed with a calm and tranquil spirit because God is your strength. He is always present to help you.

Day 3

Our Lord is blessing you with boldness and strength. Fear and doubt shall be far from you because the Lord is always with you.

SCRIPTURE READING

Have I not commanded you? Be strong and of good courage; do not be afraid, nor be dismayed, for the LORD your God is with you wherever you go.

—JOSHUA 1:9

Day 4

Our heavenly Father has blessed you with His unconditional love; His perfect love turns fear out of doors and expels every trace of terror!

Day 5

The Lord is doing a brand-new thing, and I entrust your future to Him. I pray that the fragrance of the knowledge of Jesus Christ will flow through you to others.

SCRIPTURE READING

For you, O LORD, will bless the righteous;
With favor You will surround him as with a
   shield.
—PSALM 5:12

Day 6

I ask the Lord to bless you and surround you with favor as with a shield. May He give you favor in your relationships, family and friends, teachers and schoolmates, future marriage, ministry, and career.

Day 7

I pray that you will yield yourself to our heavenly Father's plans for your life. You can do all things through Christ because He will be your strength.

SCRIPTURE READING

I bow my knees to the Father of our Lord Jesus Christ...that Christ may dwell in your hearts through faith; that you, being rooted and grounded in love, may be able...to know the love of Christ which passes knowledge; that you may be filled with all the fullness of God.
—EPHESIANS 3:14, 17, 19

Day 8

I pray that you will flourish like a stately tree. I thank God for helping you to bring forth good fruit. I pray that you will be rooted and grounded in love. May you bear godly fruit of love, joy, peace, patience, kindness, goodness, faithfulness, gentleness, and self-control.

Day 9

I thank God for flooding your mind with wisdom and creative ideas. You were created for His pleasure, and you will be transformed daily into the image and likeness of God's dear Son!

SCRIPTURE READING

Therefore, whether you eat or drink, or what-ever you do, do all to the glory of God.
—1 CORINTHIANS 10:31

Day 10

Whatever the Lord has planned for you to do, may you do it all for His glory!

Day 11

I pray that you will bless others, keeping God's ways and doing what is right and just in His sight. I pray that your offspring will be a blessing to all the nations of the earth.

SCRIPTURE READING

By Myself I have sworn, says the LORD, because you…have not withheld your son, your only son—blessing I will bless you, and in multiplying I will multiply your descendants as the stars of the heaven and as the sand which is on the seashore….In your seed all the nations of the earth shall be blessed, because you have obeyed My voice.

—GENESIS 22:16–18

Day 12

The Lord is your light and your salvation, and He will protect you from danger. With Him on your side, you are fearless, afraid of nothing and no one.

Day 13

It is our prayer that you will always seek the Lord. He will answer you, and He will deliver you from all your fears.

SCRIPTURE READING

I sought the LORD, and He heard me.
—PSALM 34:4

Day 14

I pray that you will obey God's Word and guard His teachings as you would your own eyes. Remind yourself of them; write them on your heart as if on a tablet.

Day 15

You are so very special to the Father God and to us. We believe in God, and we believe that you will know yourself and be content with who you are. Father God's strong hand is on you; He will promote you at the right time. You will learn to cast all your cares over on Him, because He is most careful with you.

SCRIPTURE READING

Therefore humble yourselves under the mighty hand of God, that He may exalt you in due time, casting all your care upon Him, for He cares for you.

—1 PETER 5:6–7

Day 16

God wants you to have a good day every day. He leads you in a plain path. Goodness, mercy, and peace are your companions in all your deliberations, and you will make wise decisions. Sometimes you must take risks, but you can trust God who watches over you.

Day 17

You are a joy to me, and I rejoice because the Lord is working out His plans for your life—for His loving-kindness continues forever. He will never abandon you—because He made you.

SCRIPTURE READING

For the weapons of our warfare are not carnal but mighty in God for pulling down strongholds, casting down arguments and every high thing that exalts itself against the knowledge of God, bringing every thought into captivity to the obedience of Christ.

—2 CORINTHIANS 10:4–5

Day 18

Little one, even before you hear ungodly ideas, I use our powerful God-tools for smashing warped philosophies and tearing down barriers you might erect against the truth of God. I fit every loose thought, emotion, and impulse into the structure of a life shaped by Christ.

Day 19

You have ears to hear God's Word, and you are learning to be obedient. You will never be self-deceived because when you hear the Word, you will be a doer of the Word.

SCRIPTURE READING

Be doers of the word, and not hearers only, deceiving yourselves.

—JAMES 1:22

Day 20

Always trust in God. You are tenderhearted. Be kind and good to others. Then you will live safely here in the land and prosper, dwelling in safety.

Day 21

I thank God that as I teach and train you up in the way that you are to go, you will receive Jesus as your personal Savior and come to know your heavenly Father.

SCRIPTURE READING

Yet in all these things we are more than conquerors through Him who loved us.

—ROMANS 8:37

Day 22

Little one, you are more than a conqueror through Christ Jesus who loves you!

Day 23

Little one, the Lord your God teaches you what is best for you. He directs you in the way you should go. I thank Father God for His promises!

SCRIPTURE READING

Thus says the LORD, your Redeemer,
The Holy One of Israel:
"I am the LORD your God...
Who leads you by the way you should go."
—ISAIAH 48:17

Day 24

Seek God and His way of doing and being right, and your ways will be pleasing to the Lord. He will make even your opponents live at peace with you.

Day 25

I pray that you will trust in the Lord and be unmoved by any circumstance.

SCRIPTURE READING

Those who trust in the LORD
Are like Mount Zion,
Which cannot be moved, but abides forever.
—PSALM 125:1

Day 26

I bless you that you might press on toward the goal to win the prize for which God has called you heavenward in Christ Jesus.

Day 27

I pray that you will let your good deeds glow for all to see, so that others will praise our heavenly Father.

SCRIPTURE READING

Who is the man that fears the LORD?
Him shall He teach in the way He chooses.
He himself shall dwell in prosperity,
And his descendants shall inherit the earth.
—PSALM 25:12–13

Day 28

I reverence God. He will teach us how to choose the best. We shall live within God's circle of blessing, and you, my child, shall inherit the earth.

Day 29

I ask the Lord to direct our work in truth, and I thank Him for establishing His covenant with us. Our descendants will be known among the nations and our offspring among the peoples. All who see them will acknowledge that they are a people the Lord has blessed.

SCRIPTURE READING

For I, the LORD, love justice....
I will direct their work in truth,
And will make with them an everlasting
    covenant....
All who see them shall acknowledge them,
That they are the posterity whom the LORD
    has blessed.

—ISAIAH 61:8–9

Day 30

The Lord has given you a heart to honor your father and mother. He will bless you with a long life, full of good things.

Day 31

I ask the Holy Spirit to show me things to come that I might train up and teach you, my child, to choose the right path. When you are older, you will remain upon it.

SCRIPTURE READING

Observe and obey all these words which I command you, that it may go well with you and your children after you forever, when you do what is good and right in the sight of the LORD your God.

—DEUTERONOMY 12:28

The Lord Is Always Present

Confessing the Powerful Truth of the Word of God

The Word of God is not just words written on a page or an account of what God did in the past. His Word is so powerful and creative that the world was framed by it. "By faith we understand that the worlds were framed by the word of God, so that the things which are seen were not made of things which are visible" (Heb. 11:3). The Word of God is creative in nature, and therefore it is still creating today.

You are using a very powerful weapon when you speak truth from the Word of God over your child. It is a quick, sharp, and powerful weapon that divides light from dark. The Word of God is called a sword in Hebrews 4:12: "For the word of God is living and powerful, and sharper than any two-edged sword, piercing even to the division of soul and spirit, and of joints and marrow, and is a discerner of the thoughts and intents of the heart."

We are not speaking mere words when we speak forth the truth of the Word of God. When we speak in agreement with God's Word, our words are spirit and life. In John 6:63, Jesus said, "It is the Spirit who gives life; the flesh profits nothing. The words that I speak to you are spirit, and they are life." When we speak the truth of the Bible, we are speaking the Word of God as revealed by His Son, Jesus Christ. His words become our words. Those words that we speak are therefore spirit and life. His words that are being spoken through us are quick, powerful, and sharper than any double-edged sword.

Jesus, the Lord and Savior we serve, is the Truth. "Jesus said to him, 'I am the way, the truth, and the life'" (John 14:6). All authority of heaven and earth has been given to Jesus Christ, and you are a joint heir with Him. When you speak His Word of truth, your words carry the weight of the authority of His kingdom, His Word, and His unchangeable promises.

The word of truth that is near, in your mouth, and in your heart is powerful. As you agree with the truth of the Word of God and speak blessings over your child, you are speaking in Christ in the sight of God. He will watch over His Word, and He will perform it. His Word will never wither or fade away, God's Word is sure and stands forever. "The grass withers, the flower fades, but the word of our God stands forever" (Isa. 40:8).

Day 1

I ask God to guard you from every evil. He will guard you when you leave and when you return. He is guarding you now, and He will guard you always. The Lord will watch over your coming and going both now and forever.

SCRIPTURE READING

The LORD shall preserve you from all evil;
He shall preserve your soul.
The LORD shall preserve your going out and
  your coming in
From this time forth, and even forevermore.
—PSALM 121:7–8

Day 2

I thank Father God for going with you wherever you are today. I ask Him to guard you as you pursue His life that He conferred as a gift through Jesus. I thank Him for posting a night watch about you each night.

Day 3

God is your Guardian, and He is right at your side to protect you. He won't fall asleep, and He will keep you from stumbling.

SCRIPTURE READING

We know that whoever is born of God does not sin; but he who has been born of God keeps himself, and the wicked one does not touch him.

—1 JOHN 5:18

Day 4

God will keep your life, little one. He has written in the Bible long ago many things that will teach you patience and keep you encouraged.

Day 5

In the name of Jesus, I bless you with the benefits He has bestowed on you. His plans are perfect, and in the fullness of time we will understand what eye has not seen and ear has not heard. He is keeping them ready for you.

SCRIPTURE READING

Eye has not seen, nor ear heard, nor have entered into the heart of man the things which God has prepared for those who love Him.
—1 CORINTHIANS 2:9

Day 6

You are blessed with His promise that preserves your life. The Lord will bless your coming in and going out.

Day 7

Little one, you are blessed, for the Father God is always watching over you; He never sleeps. He cares for you, defends you, and protects you day and night.

Scripture Reading

Now to Him who is able to keep you from
    stumbling,
And to present you faultless
Before the presence of His glory with exceed-
    ing joy,
To God our Savior,
Who alone is wise,
Be glory and majesty,
Dominion and power,
Both now and forever.
Amen.

—Jude 24–25

Day 8

All glory to God, who is able to keep you from stumbling. He will bring you into His glorious presence with great joy.

Day 9

Precious one, you are most blessed. Wherever you walk, God's Word will guide you; whenever you rest, it will guard you. His blessings are upon you, and He will always hold you by the hand and guide you.

SCRIPTURE READING

If any of you lacks wisdom, let him ask of God, who gives to all liberally and without reproach, and it will be given to him. But let him ask in faith, with no doubting, for he who doubts is like a wave of the sea driven and tossed by the wind.

—JAMES 1:5–6

Day 10

The Father and I will teach you to ask for His wisdom when you don't know what to do. He gives generously to all without finding fault, and it will be given to you.

Day 11

I pray that you will delight in the ways of our God, and then you will walk with firm steps. May God have a good grip on your hand.

SCRIPTURE READING

For You are my rock and my fortress;
Therefore, for Your name's sake,
Lead me and guide me…
For You are my strength.

—PSALM 31:3–4

Day 12

God is instructing you and teaching you in the way you should go. He commissioned me to train you in this way of life and instruct you in the practice of all He has commanded. He will always be with you, loving you and counseling you with His eye upon you.

Day 13

I thank our Lord God for being a sun and shield. You have been blessed with His favor and honor. He is not withholding any good thing from you.

SCRIPTURE READING

For the LORD God is a sun and shield;
The LORD will give grace and glory;
No good thing will He withhold
From those who walk uprightly.

—PSALM 84:11

Day 14

I thank the Lord for keeping you when you are going out and when you are coming in. He gives rest to those He loves. My child, you are His best gift to me—His generous legacy.

Day 15

The Lord is always present to keep you constantly renewed in the spirit of your mind (having a fresh mental and spiritual attitude). You will grow in understanding and put on the new nature (the regenerate self) created in His image (the godlike self), in true righteousness and holiness.

Scripture Reading

Be renewed in the spirit of your mind, and ... put on the new man which was created according to God, in true righteousness and holiness.
—Ephesians 4:23–24

Day 16

Little one, the Lord will keep you safe. God has blessed you to be a person of understanding who delights in wisdom.

Day 17

From this time on and forevermore, God loves you and keeps you, little one.

SCRIPTURE READING

God is faithful, by whom you were called into the fellowship of His Son, Jesus Christ our Lord.

—1 CORINTHIANS 1:9

Day 18

I thank our Father God for keeping us today. God has blessed you by calling you into companionship and participation with His Son, Jesus Christ our Lord.

Day 19

From this time on and forevermore, He who keeps you will not slumber or sleep. I thank Him for His faithfulness to you each evening as you sleep.

SCRIPTURE READING

My help comes from the LORD,
Who made heaven and earth.
He will not allow your foot to be moved;
He who keeps you will not slumber.
Behold, He who keeps Israel
Shall neither slumber nor sleep.

—PSALM 121:2–4

Day 20

Little one, God has revealed His Word to us that we might obey it. He will keep us safe.

Day 21

God is blessing you and teaching you to love what is good. He will keep your life joyful, and His love for you will never fail or quit.

SCRIPTURE READING

You love righteousness and hate wickedness;
Therefore God, Your God, has anointed You
With the oil of gladness more than Your
   companions.

—PSALM 45:7

Day 22

The Lord will keep your going out and your coming in, little one. I proclaim that you will enjoy the fruits of your labors, for these are gifts from God.

Day 23

I thank Father God for making provision for you. Little one, always believe in the Lord Jesus, and you will be saved—you and your household.

SCRIPTURE READING

Believe on the Lord Jesus Christ, and you will be saved, you and your household.

—ACTS 16:31

Day 24

I thank our heavenly Father for pouring out His love into you by the Holy Spirit. For God loved you so much that He gave His only Son so that when you believe in Him, you shall not perish but have eternal life.

Day 25

I thank our everlasting Father that you keep His Word. Because you keep His Word in passionate patience, He will keep you safe in the times of testing. May you keep a tight grip on what you have so that no one distracts you.

SCRIPTURE READING

Whom have I in heaven but You?
And there is none upon earth that I desire
    besides You.
My flesh and my heart fail;
But God is the strength of my heart and my
    portion forever.

—PSALM 73:25–26

Day 26

May Father God bless you to stay in His refreshing presence. God is with you always, even to the end of the world.

Day 27

Father God has blessed you with His promise for salvation that preserves your life. Let the name of the Lord be praised, both now and forevermore. God is your refuge and strength. He is ever present.

SCRIPTURE READING

Blessed be the name of the LORD
From this time forth and forevermore!
From the rising of the sun to its going down
The LORD's name is to be praised.

—PSALM 113:2–3

Day 28

The Lord God has said that He will cause all His goodness to pass in front of you, and He will proclaim His name, the Lord, so you can hear it. May the Lord have mercy and compassion on you today and forevermore.

Day 29

My precious child, your times are in the Lord's hands. He will deliver you from your opponents and from those who would pursue you wrongly. He will cause His face to shine on you, saving you in His unfailing love.

SCRIPTURE READING

My times are in Your hand;
Deliver me from the hand of my enemies,
And from those who persecute me.
Make Your face shine upon Your servant;
Save me for Your mercies' sake.

—PSALM 31:15–16

Day 30

I thank the Lord God of heaven, the great and awesome God, for keeping His covenant of unfailing love toward you. His eyes are open to hear the prayer that His servants are praying before Him day and night. I thank Him for blessing your going out and your coming in.

Knowing Jesus

Rejoice

It is God's will for your joy and your child's joy to be full. Many times we settle for a limited amount of joy because we have allowed ourselves to become accustomed to listening to the voice of defeat and worry. The Word of God has been given to us so that our joy will be full. "And these things we write to you that your joy may be full" (1 John 1:4). Meditating on the Word of Truth, the goodness of God, His promises, His testimonies, His nature, His fullness, His authority, and His love will bring untold joy in your life. The worries of this life will begin to drop off and be replaced with joy, confidence, and faith when you put on the mind of Christ.

This is a wonderful time of celebration because we are rejoicing in God's gift to us, His Son, Jesus Christ. His life on earth is our example. Because He knew no sin, He was the perfect offering for our sins. During His life on earth, He only did what He saw His Father in heaven doing. His will was completely bound to the will of God. His love for us was over-flowing, while at the same time His eyes were fixed on heaven and the purpose He was sent forth to do.

Keep in mind and close to your heart that God's love for you and for your little one has no boundaries. "And I pray that you, being rooted and established in love, may have power, together with all the saints, to grasp how wide and long and high and deep is the love of Christ, and to know this love that surpasses knowledge—that you may be filled to the measure of all the fullness of God" (Eph. 3:17–19, NIV).

It is impossible for you to comprehend how wide, how long, how high, and how deep His love is for you and your baby. When the Father God looks at you, He sees the life of His Son because we are alive and made new creatures in Him. God the Father loved you so much that He gave His own Son for you. He bruised His own Son for you. "Yet it pleased the LORD to bruise Him; He has put Him to grief" (Isa. 53:10).

God bruised His Son for you because your redemption and fullness of joy is His will for you. Jesus came to earth as a gift to you, and even though He was completely sinless, He was made sin for you so that in Him you could become the righteousness of God. "For He made Him who knew no sin to be sin for us, that we might become the righteousness of God in Him" (2 Cor. 5:21).

Jesus came so that you and your child could have abundant, eternal life. Never question God's love for you. All of His promises are fulfilled in Christ Jesus. Because of Him, all of His promises are "yes and amen" to you. This is the reason why He gave

Himself as a sacrifice for you. Even during times of sorrow and tribulation, there is reason to rejoice. If you are living in Him, you are fellowshiping with His sufferings during times of trial and persecution. This intimate fellowship with His sufferings is actually a time to rejoice and be glad about all He has done and all He is about to do.

Let the bells of your heart rejoice. Let the trumpet of your voice announce His praises. Open wide your mouth to shout and sing the truth of His Word. And let the tenderness of your arms embrace your little one as you declare the truth of His Word that reigns forevermore!

Day 1

I thank our heavenly Father for loving you so much that He gave you Jesus. Jesus is your wonderful Counselor, mighty God, everlasting Father, and Prince of Peace.

SCRIPTURE READING

For unto us a Child is born,
Unto us a Son is given;
And the government will be upon His
    shoulder.
And His name will be called
Wonderful, Counselor, Mighty God,
Everlasting Father, Prince of Peace.
—ISAIAH 9:6–7

Day 2

This day our mighty God has fed us like a good shepherd. I thank Him for keeping us. He has gathered us in His arms and carried us in His bosom. We feel safe as He gently leads those of us who have young children.

Day 3

"*Glory to God* in the heavenly heights, peace to all men and women on earth who please You." Just as Mary did, I will treasure the things God reveals to me about your future and think about them. May you be an imitator of the One who loves you.

SCRIPTURE READING

> Then the angel said to them, "Do not be afraid, for behold, I bring you good tidings of great joy which will be to all people. For there is born to you this day in the city of David a Savior, who is Christ the Lord."
>
> —LUKE 2:10–11

Day 4

You belong to God, and you are an heir with Christ. I thank Him for choosing you that you may set forth the wonderful deeds and display the virtues and perfections of Him who called us out of darkness into His marvelous light.

Day 5

I bless you to be an imitator of Jesus. You will follow me as I follow Jesus. My prayer is that you will always do what pleases God.

SCRIPTURE READING

And He who sent Me is with Me. The Father has not left Me alone, for I always do those things that please Him.

—JOHN 8:29

Day 6

Listen, my child; I read to you the message God sent, the good news of peace through Jesus Christ, who is Lord of all. Jesus is anointed with the Holy Spirit and power, leaving us as witnesses of His good deeds.

Day 7

I pray to our Father in heaven that you will have the compassion of Jesus. May you be moved by compassion and bless others.

SCRIPTURE READING

But You are God,
Ready to pardon,
Gracious and merciful,
Slow to anger,
Abundant in kindness,
And did not forsake them.

—NEHEMIAH 9:17

Day 8

I pray that you will be clothed in kindness. As an imitator of Christ, you will be gracious and merciful, slow to anger, and abundant in kindness.

Day 9

Unto us was born a Savior, a wonderful Counselor, a mighty God, an everlasting Father, and a Prince of Peace. I receive Jesus, and I purpose to lead you according to His example. He gave you the right to become a child of God.

Scripture Reading

And this is the testimony: that God has given us eternal life, and this life is in His Son. He who has the Son has life; he who does not have the Son of God does not have life.

—1 John 5:11–12

Day 10

I pray that when you are older, you will believe that Jesus is the Messiah. For to us, certainly a Child has been born, and this Child is Jesus. The eternal life that God has given to us is in the Son, and whoever believes in the Son has life.

Day 11

I thank Father God that He is making known to you the path of life. This is a life filled with joy in His presence, with eternal pleasures at every turn. You shall call Him the everlasting Father and the Prince of Peace.

SCRIPTURE READING

You will show me the path of life;
In Your presence is fullness of joy;
At Your right hand are pleasures forevermore.
—PSALM 16:11

Day 12

Before the Lord, I bless you today, my child, with a promise from Him that there is hope in this world. I thank Him for the riches of the glory of the mystery, which is Christ within and among us, the hope of [realizing the] glory.

Day 13

Little one, rest assured that you can take courage when you hold on to God's promise with confidence. This confidence is like a strong and trustworthy anchor for your soul.

Scripture Reading

> This hope we have as an anchor of the soul, both sure and steadfast, and which enters the Presence behind the veil, where the forerunner has entered for us, even Jesus, having become High Priest forever.
> —Hebrews 6:19–20

Day 14

I thank our Lord God that you will seriously live the new resurrection life with Christ. May you pursue Christlike things and see things from His perspective. Jesus is our new life in God. You are God's workmanship, created in Christ Jesus to do good works. God has prepared projects in advance for you to do. You will do all these as unto the Lord.

Day 15

Little one, you are justified through faith and have peace with God through Jesus. Jesus is the Prince of Peace, and we rejoice in the hope of the glory of God.

SCRIPTURE READING

Therefore, having been justified by faith, we have peace with God through our Lord Jesus Christ, through whom also we have access by faith into this grace in which we stand, and rejoice in hope of the glory of God.

—ROMANS 5:1–2

Day 16

I pray that you will walk as Jesus walked. May you clothe yourself with humility, for He gives grace to the humble. I pray that you will walk in self-confidence because Jesus is your Lord.

Day 17

Little one, I pray that whatever you do or say, it will be as a representative of the Lord Jesus, and together we will give thanks through Him to God the Father.

SCRIPTURE READING

And whatever you do in word or deed, do all in the name of the Lord Jesus, giving thanks to God the Father through Him.

—COLOSSIANS 3:17

Day 18

Little one, our heavenly Father knew you before He made the world, and He decided that you would be like His Son.

Day 19

I just want to thank our everlasting Father for giving us the victory through our Lord Jesus Christ. I thank Him for the marvelous changes in our lives.

Scripture Reading

That He would grant you, according to the riches of His glory, to be strengthened with might through His Spirit in the inner man.

—Ephesians 3:16

Day 20

As we rest tonight, we will glory in the Lord's love. I thank Him that through His Holy Spirit and by faith we have strength and power in our inner beings. We are learning of the height and depth of His great love for us.

Day 21

My precious child, God has given you a strong heart that is full of courage and tenacity. It is delightful to watch you learn new things about yourself every day! I purpose to train you up in the Word of God so that you will keep your direction toward the final goal. Inwardly, you are being renewed every day.

SCRIPTURE READING

Therefore we do not lose heart. Even though our outward man is perishing, yet the inward man is being renewed day by day.
—2 CORINTHIANS 4:16

Day 22

I bless you daily with the food of faith and love. May you be filled with hope for the word of truth, for the gospel is your mainstay. The Prince of Peace is your companion and strength for this day.

Day 23

I purpose to teach you, my child, in a spirit of profound common sense so that I can begin to bring you to maturity. I pray that you will use the divine energy God generously gives you to do your very best.

SCRIPTURE READING

Who Himself bore our sins in His own body on the tree, that we, having died to sins, might live for righteousness—by whose stripes you were healed.

—1 PETER 2:24

Day 24

I thank God for this beautiful Christmas Eve. I rejoice that our heavenly Father gave us His Son, Jesus. I thank Jesus for bearing our sins on the cross so that we could live unto righteousness. By His stripes we were healed.

Day 25

Little one, we are passing on to you our tradition of celebrating Christmas, the day chosen to honor our Lord's birth. We pray that you will follow in our footsteps and set aside this time as holy. Jesus is the Word that came to earth and lived among us. In the beginning He was with God, and He was God. He is full of grace and truth, and from Him we receive one gift after another. We give Jesus all that we have—we give Him ourselves.

SCRIPTURE READING

And the Word became flesh and dwelt among us, and we beheld His glory, the glory as of the only begotten of the Father, full of grace and truth.

—JOHN 1:14

Day 26

Together we thank Father God for the birth of His Son. His name is Jesus—"God saves"—because He will save His people from their sins. He is also called "Emmanuel," which is Hebrew for "God is with us."

Day 27

May you inherit a willingness to be in agreement with your godly parents and caregivers. In the name of our Lord Jesus Christ, I pray that we will be completely joined together by having the same kind of thinking and the same purpose. I bind our minds to the mind of Christ that we may hold the thoughts, feelings, and purposes of His heart.

SCRIPTURE READING

Therefore we also pray always for you that our God would count you worthy of this calling, and fulfill all the good pleasure of His goodness and the work of faith with power, that the name of our Lord Jesus Christ may be glorified in you, and you in Him, according to the grace of our God and the Lord Jesus Christ.

—2 THESSALONIANS 1:11–12

Day 28

Little one, you are blessed, for Father God is always with you. Whatever you do in word or deed, do it all in the name of Jesus, giving thanks to God and the Father by Him.

Day 29

I thank the Prince of Peace for being with you today. I thank Him for the reality of knowing that He loves you, and that you will know that you are loved. May you be secure in the blessings of His love, believing that Jesus is the Christ, and may you share this godly love with others.

SCRIPTURE READING

And this is His commandment: that we should believe on the name of His Son Jesus Christ and love one another, as He gave us commandment.

—1 JOHN 3:23

Day 30

Our precious child, I thank God that Jesus is your example. You will be blessed as you grow in wisdom and in stature. Just as Jesus did, you will grow in favor with God and men. Jesus is our wonderful Counselor, the mighty God, the everlasting Father, the Prince of Peace.

Day 31

I pray that you will rejoice in God our Savior. His name is majestic in all the earth! I thank God that you are of one heart and one mind with Him. You are learning to believe that Jesus was sent by God to save the world. I bless you with His love for you.

SCRIPTURE READING

I do not pray for these alone, but also for those who will believe in Me through their word; that they all may be one, as You, Father, are in Me, and I in You; that they also may be one in Us, that the world may believe that You sent Me. And the glory which You gave Me I have given them, that they may be one just as We are one: I in them, and You in Me; that they may be made perfect in one, and that the world may know that You have sent Me, and have loved them as You have loved Me.

—JOHN 17:20–23

About the Author

Germaine Copeland, president and founder of Word Ministries, Inc., is an anointed conference speaker and the best-selling author of the Prayers That Avail Much® book series. There are currently more than three million copies in print.

Please send correspondence to Germaine Copeland at:

Word Ministries, Inc.
38 Sloan Street
Roswell, Georgia 30076

You can also visit her Web site at www.prayers.org.

Strang Communications, the publisher of both Charisma House and *Charisma* magazine, wants to give you a FREE SUBSCRIPTION to our award-winning magazine.

Since its inception in 1975, *Charisma* magazine has helped thousands of Christians stay connected with what God is doing worldwide.

Within its pages you will discover in-depth reports and the latest news from a Christian perspective, biblical health tips, global events in the body of Christ, personality profiles, and so much more. Join the family of *Charisma* readers who enjoy feeding their spirit each month with miracle-filled testimonies and inspiring articles that bring clarity, provoke prayer, and demand answers.

To claim your **3 free issues** of *Charisma*, send your name and address to: Charisma 3 Free Issue Offer, 600 Rinehart Road, Lake Mary, FL 32746. Or you may call 1-800-829-3346 and ask for Offer # 93FREE. This offer is only valid in the USA.

---

www.charismamag.com